Android Arcade
Game App

J. F. DiMarzio

Apress·

Android Arcade Game App

ISBN-13 (pbk): 978-1-4302-4545-2

ISBN-13 (electronic): 978-1-4302-4546-9

President and Publisher: Paul Manning
Lead Editor: Steve Anglin
Development Editor: Tom Welsh
Technical Reviewer: Tony Hillerson
Editorial Board: Steve Anglin, Ewan Buckingham, Gary Cornell, Louise Corrigan, Morgan Ertel, Jonathan Gennick, Jonathan Hassell, Robert Hutchinson, Michelle Lowman, James Markham, Matthew Moodie, Jeff Olson, Jeffrey Pepper, Douglas Pundick, Ben Renow-Clarke, Dominic Shakeshaft, Gwenan Spearing, Matt Wade, Tom Welsh
Coordinating Editor: Katie Sullivan
Copy Editor: Kimberly Burton
Compositor: SPi Global
Indexer: SPi Global
Artist: SPi Global
Cover Designer: Anna Ishchenko

Distributed to the book trade worldwide by Springer Science+Business Media New York, 233 Spring Street, 6th Floor, New York, NY 10013. Phone 1-800-SPRINGER, fax (201) 348-4505, e-mail orders-ny@springer-sbm.com, or visit www.springeronline.com.

For information on translations, please e-mail rights@apress.com, or visit www.apress.com.

Apress and friends of ED books may be purchased in bulk for academic, corporate, or promotional use. eBook versions and licenses are also available for most titles. For more information, reference our Special Bulk Sales–eBook Licensing web page at www.apress.com/bulk-sales.

Any source code or other supplementary materials referenced by the author in this text is available to readers at www.apress.com. For detailed information about how to locate your book's source code, go to www.apress.com/source-code/.

Thank you to Suzannah, Christian, Sophia, and Giovanni for always being there.

–J. F. DiMarzio

Contents at a Glance

Contents

About the Author

J. F. DiMarzio is a game developer and web professional. He has more than twenty years of experience in technology and design. Having authored eleven books, he is a leading resource in Android and Android game development.

Currently, Mr. DiMarzio is a developer for the Walt Disney Company. He resides in Central Florida with his wife, Suzannah, and three children. Suzannah's blog is at zannaland.com.

About the Technical Reviewer

Tony Hillerson is a mobile developer and cofounder at Tack Mobile. He graduated from Ambassador University with a bachelor's degree in Management Information Systems. On any given day, he may be working with Objective-C, Java, Ruby, CoffeeScript, JavaScript, HTML, or shell scripts. Tony has spoken at RailsConf, AnDevCon, and 360|Flex. He is the creator of the popular O'Reilly Android screencasts.

In his free time, Tony enjoys playing the bass and Warr Guitar, and making electronic music. Tony lives outside Denver, Colorado, with his wife, Lori, and sons, Titus and Lincoln.

About the Game Graphics Designer

Ben Eagle has been working with computer graphics and web development for 14 years, which he learned while serving in the Marine Corps. While working with various companies, Ben has designed hundreds of sites, company signs, logos, commercials, and marketing graphics. Currently he works as a senior programmer, living in Davenport Florida. At the age of 34 he continues to pursue his career and teaches graphics to students on the side. He has acquired two associate's degrees in digital media and web development. Ben also has his MCP and C++/Java certification. In his leisure he continues his passion in computer arts and programming and performs in a band.

Acknowledgments

The author would like to acknowledge his agent, Neil Salkind, as well as Steve, Katie, Tom, Tony, Kim, and the gang at Apress.

Chapter 1

Introduction to Android Gaming

Welcome to *Android Arcade Game App*. In this book, you will learn how to create an Android arcade-style game "from project to publish." While I will walk you through solutions to some gaming development problems, this book is not necessarily for beginner developers.

You chose this book because you are passionate about Android as a platform and you want to develop arcade-style, Android-based games. By the time you have finished reading this book, you will have the knowledge you need to create a fun and compelling game on Android's latest flavor: Ice Cream Sandwich. The advantage of this is that the games you build in this book will run on both Android-based phones and Android tablets.

It is hugely satisfying to sit down and play a game that you wrote. This is especially true of arcade games, which lend themselves perfectly to the casual mobile gamer experience.

What You Should Know

Before reading this book, you should have a good working knowledge of Android development. This means that you are well-versed in Java and the Android SDK, and you have tried your hand at building projects and applications in Android.

You should also be familiar with the Eclipse IDE (integrated development environment). While Android games can be developed in many different IDEs, all of the examples in this book use Eclipse Indigo. If you do not have a current version of Eclipse, download it from `http://eclipse.org`.

> **Note**   While it is possible to debug your code using the emulator, get an Android device if you are serious about game development. I have found that the emulator does not always render as accurately or run as fast as a mobile device running a comparable SDK level. And when you are writing a game, accuracy is key.

Finally, you should have at least beginner-level knowledge of game development to get the most out of this book. You may never have written a game on your own, but you should know what it takes to develop one. What this means, in practice, is that you should have a basic knowledge of OpenGL ES and how it is used in Android gaming.

In creating the Prison Break game in this book, you will use `gl0rthof()`, GLSurfaceView, textures, vertices, and other OpenGL ES concepts. If none of these sound familiar to you, I suggest you start with a more entry-level book, such as *Practical Android 4 Game Development* by J. F. DiMarzio (Apress, 2011).

What You Will Learn

In this book, you will learn how to use your knowledge of Android development and OpenGL ES to create an entertaining, interesting game. You will build a game that follows the conventions of the arcade style. The game, Prison Break, includes many of the elements of more complicated games—thus making it a good learning tool.

By the end of this book, you will have learned key programming skills for developing arcade-style Android games. The following is a list (in no particular order) of some of the skills that you will pick up as you progress through this book:

- Displaying and manipulating graphics with OpenGL
- Working with resources such as bitmaps
- Spawning and killing Android threads
- Creating a splash screen, a menu system, and a game engine

A Brief History of Gaming

While mobile games have been around for hundreds of years in one form or another (everything from card games to dice), the genesis of modern, popular, mobile video gaming can be traced back to the Nintendo Game Boy. The Game Boy may not have been the first and it may not have been the best, but it did make every kid, teenager, and some adults want to walk around playing *Tetris* and *Super Mario*; feats that until then could only be accomplished on large consoles that still had the stigma of being "a child's toy."

> **Note**   It is generally accepted that the first mobile gaming device was actually the Microvision, which was released in 1979. Nintendo's Game Boy, however, brought mobile gaming to the masses, and popularized it as a viable gaming platform.

The Nintendo Game Boy featured a small, gray-scale screen and interchangeable games. Until this time, the majority of portable "video games" were single-function devices that played either one or a small set of preinstalled games. But people could finally take their video games, albeit scaled-downed versions, anywhere they wanted to. This put mobile games in the hands of the masses, but what about the developers?

While there was an established base of casual or independent computer game developers at the time, the Game Boy was not a practical platform for them because it was still considered a gaming console. Games were developed using proprietary C libraries and required the use of expensive, licensed, development hardware. This put development out of reach of the casual game developers, relegating them to PCs if they wanted to express themselves.

Around the same time the Game Boy was hitting its stride, two more revolutions began to take form; revolutions that would lead us to Android as a gaming platform. Cell phones and the Internet began to become widely used and accepted by the late 1980s, just as portable gaming took off.

Early mobile phones were expensive to make and expensive to use. They were toys for the rich and famous, and tools for the successful who wanted to show off. The screens on these devices consisted of a single line of LCD text; just enough to display the phone number being dialed. The idea of a business tycoon or Hollywood producer sitting down to play *Tetris* on a single-line display at anywhere from $15 to $25 per minute was simply not practical. It would take a few more years before mobile-phone displays and per-minute rates would allow for gaming.

It wasn't long after cell phones and the Internet became popular that the two collided. At first, the marriage of the two produced crude, scaled-down versions of web-like content that could easily run on the cell phone's slow processors and limited—mostly textual—displays. Slowly, mobile Java-based content and applications began to pop up on cell phones everywhere. Although this added the overhead of a Java virtual machine, it was definitely a good start. The first Java-based games followed shortly thereafter.

Nokia finally attempted to fully merge cell phones with mobile gaming devices with its N*Gage phone in 2003. The N*Gage, while generally viewed as a commercial failure, opened the door to cell phone gaming as a true multiplatform activity. Developers soon realized that games built specifically to run on mobile phones could actually compete with those built for gaming-specific handheld systems like the Game Boy, PSP, and DS.

Mobile gaming finally found consumer acceptance with the iPhone. There is no denying that the iPhone did not just open the door for mobile phone–based games, it blew the door away. This does not mean that the iPhone is without fault. Developing iPhone games requires two things that not every casual developer may possess: a Mac and a very good understanding of Objective-C.

This is where Android picks up the story.

The Introduction of Android

I began developing on the Android beta platform in early 2008. At the time, no phones were announced for the new operating system and we—as developers—genuinely felt as though we were in at the start of something exciting. Android captured all of the energy and excitement of the early days of open-source development. Developing for the platform was very reminiscent of sitting around an empty student lounge at 2:00 am with a Jolt Cola, waiting for VAX time to run our latest code. It was an exciting platform. I am glad I was there to see it materialize and take off.

As Android began to grow, and as Google released more updates to solidify the final architecture, one thing became apparent: Android, based on Java and including many well-known Java packages, would be an easy transition for the casual game developer. Most of the knowledge that an existing Java developer already had could be recycled on this new platform. The very large base of Java game developers could use that knowledge to move fairly smoothly onto Android.

So how does one begin developing games on Android? What tools are required? The next section of this chapter aims to answer these questions.

Android Game Programming

Developing games on Android has its pros and cons. You should be aware of these before you begin. First, Android games are developed in Java, but it is not full Java. Many of the packages that you may have used for OpenGL and other graphic blandishments are included in the Android SDK. Many does not mean *all*, however, and some packages that are very helpful to game developers, especially 3D game developers, are not included. So not every package that you may have relied on to build your previous games will be available to you in Android.

With each release of new Android SDKs, more and more packages become available. You will need to be aware of just which packages you have to work with. We will cover these as we progress through the chapters.

Another pro (and a corresponding con) have to do with Android's familiarity versus its lack of power. What Android gains in familiarity and ease of programming, it may lack in speed and power. Most video games, like those written for PCs or consoles, are developed in low-level languages such as C and even Assembly. This gives the developers the most control over how the code is executed by the processor and the environment in which the code is run. Processors, of course, only understand machine code, and the closer you can get to their native language, the fewer interpreters you need to jump through to get your game running. Android, while it does offer some limited ability to code at a low level, interprets and threads your Java code through its own execution system. This gives the developer less control over the environment the game is run in.

This book is not going to take you through the low-level approaches to game development. Why not? Because Java, especially as it is presented for general Android development, is widely known, easy to use, and can make some very engaging and rewarding games.

In essence, if you are already an experienced Java developer, you will find that your skills are not lost in translation when applied to Android. If you are not already a seasoned Java developer, do not fear. Java is a great language to start your learning. For this reason, I have chosen to stick with Android's native Java development environment to write our games.

We have discussed a couple of pros and a couple of cons to developing games on Android. One of the best reasons for independent and casual game developers to create and publish games on the Android platform is the freedom granted in releasing your games. While some app stores have very stringent rules about what can be sold on them—and for how much—the Android Market does not. Anyone is free to list and sell just about anything he or she wants. This gives developers more creative freedom.

Now that we have quickly reviewed the history of mobile gaming and discussed some of the reasons why you might want to put your valuable time and effort into developing games on the Android network, it's time to take a look at the tools you need to be a successful Android game developer.

Summary

In this chapter, you discovered what you will learn in this book. You were introduced to the history of mobile gaming and the Android gaming platform. In the next chapter, you learn what constitutes an arcade-style game and what makes these games so playable on Android devices.

Chapter 2

What Is an Arcade Game?

In this chapter, you will learn what defines a game as an arcade-style game. You will also form an operational definition of arcade-style gaming.

As the chapter comes to a close, you discover more about Prison Break, the game that you will create in the remaining chapters of the book.

Where Did Arcade-Style Games Originate?

There are many styles of games in the gaming world today. From first-person shooters to puzzle games to multigame hybrids, there are arguably as many styles as there are games to play. Games such as *N.O.V.A. 2* and *Words with Friends* are great examples of these mobile games.

One of the most popular game styles right now is arcade. Arcade games, as a style, are really hybrids that encompass many different game styles. To understand what an arcade-style game is, let's take a quick look at the history of arcade gaming.

No doubt, you have seen—either in person or online—an old arcade game cabinet like *Pac-Man* or *Centipede*. In the early days, gaming hardware was expensive and was typically customized for every game. Developers worked hand in hand with hardware creators, which resulted in very large, furniture-like, game cabinets.

These large, all-in-one cabinets typically contained a monitor, a controller, and all of the internal electronics needed to run the game. Because these units were prohibitively expensive, however, the average person could not afford to buy one; so they were usually found only in video-game arcades. The cabinets were fitted with coin accepters and people eagerly fed quarters into them to play the latest titles. Therefore, the root of the name for the "arcade" game style comes from the place where the games were originally played.

Arcade owners quickly learned one thing: in order to recoup the high costs of buying the game machines, they needed as many players as possible to play each game. Today, people can play a single game for hours at a time. I have been known to log 10, 20, or even 30 hours into a *Final Fantasy* game. This type of hardcore gaming would have spelled doom for arcade owners at $.25 per play.

Arcade owners and game developers quickly realized that three minutes was the magic number. At an average game-time of three minutes, gamers felt they got their quarter's worth, and arcade owners could move a lot of players through the game.

Game developers now had to create games that a player could walk up to, understand the gameplay and objectives without any instruction, and stop playing after three minutes. Thus began the development of games that were addictive, had a clearly defined objective, and could be played in a relatively short amount of time. These are the origins of the arcade-style game.

In the next section of this chapter, we discuss the game that you will develop in this book.

Your Game: Prison Break

In the book's remaining chapters, you learn how to create an arcade-style game called Prison Break. Prison Break is a paddle game that involves deflecting the trajectory of a ball into a wall of bricks in order to break them. The game is loosely based on the game *Breakout* by Atari. *Breakout* was a very influential game in the early days of arcade gaming, and its addictive gameplay and easy-to-understand concept makes it a perfect example for this book.

Prison Break contains all of the elements needed to build a good, game development knowledge base. You will learn about polygon and texture rendering, basic game physics, and collision detection. These are all concepts that you will undoubtedly use in other games.

This book will walk you through the development of Prison Break in a natural order, from beginning to end. You will be provided with code samples and explanations for creating the game and playing it on your Android device. By the end of the book, you will have gained the knowledge you need to easily create other games based on the same concepts. Figure 2-1 illustrates a scene from the completed Prison Break.

Figure 2-1. A screenshot from the completed Prison Break

To give you a clear idea of what lies ahead, the next section lays out the content and goals of the remaining chapters.

In This Book...

There are eight chapters in this book. And while the overall book may seem short in length, it is going to be packed with a lot of useful information. Each chapter aims to equip you with one key skill needed to complete the Prison Break game. What follows is a brief overview of the goals of our six remaining chapters.

Chapter 3: Creating a Menu

In this chapter, you learn how to create the menu system for Prison Break. The menu of the game is the main entry point, which guides the player into and out of Prison Break. You will create options for starting and exiting the game using the Android SDK.

Chapter 4: Drawing the Background

Chapter 4 teaches you how to create a background for the game and draw that background to the screen. In the process, you are introduced to many aspects of OpenGL ES, including rendering, texture mapping, and vertices. The background, while static for the Prison Break game, sets the theme for each game you create, and is, therefore, very important.

Chapter 5: Creating the Player Paddle and Bricks

In Chapter 5, you learn how to create a paddle that is moved across the screen based on where the player directs the character. You also add the ball that is used to break the bricks. This involves the use of touch listeners and custom classes in Android.

To finish this chapter, you create the bricks that the player character needs to bust through to advance through the game. You will learn how to use Android code loops to place multiple blocks on the screen without having to draw them manually.

Chapter 6: Collision Detection and In-Game Physics

Chapter 6 walks you through the critical concept of collision detection. The physics of collision detection is used to tell if the brick-breaking ball has hit a brick (or the paddle). You then use physics and mathematics to either bounce the ball in a new direction or destroy a brick. It is this in-game physics that adds realism to your game and makes it enjoyable to play.

Chapter 7: Keeping Score

While it can be overlooked and considered simplistic, the ability to keep score is very important to many arcade-style games. Chapter 7 teaches you how to keep track of the current game score and how to save the score to one of Android's built-in MySQL databases.

Chapter 8: Adding More Levels

In Chapter 8, you learn how to add levels to the game. An exciting aspect of designing arcade-style games is that you can add many levels—sometimes hundreds of them—quickly and easily. You will apply the knowledge you gained from previous chapters to create multiple levels for your game.

Summary

In this chapter, you learned what defines an arcade game; you discovered more about Prison Break, the game that you will create; and you got a brief overview of the remaining chapters of this book.

In Chapter 3, you begin coding your game's main menu screen.

Chapter 3

Creating a Menu

In this chapter, you will create a two-part menu screen for your Prison Break game. The menu screen, shown in Figure 3-1, is made up of two different "screens" containing a total of five different images.

Figure 3-1. *Prison Break menu screen*

In the next section, you will learn what you need to do to prepare for the code provided in this chapter.

Before You Begin

Before you begin to apply the code in this chapter, there are two things you need to do to prepare. First, create a new Android project named `prisonbreak`. This project will hold all of the code and images used in this book.

Second, gather or create some images for your Prison Break game. In this chapter, you need a total of five images: a splash screen, two different Start button states, and two different Exit button states. The images that I used are shown in Figures 3-2 through 3-6.

Figure 3-2. prisonbreaksplash.png

Figure 3-3. startbtn.png

Figure 3-4. startbtndown.png

Figure 3-5. exitbtn.png

Figure 3-6. exitbtndown.png

If you have never worked with graphics or images in Android, I have a couple of valuable tips. First, you can work with images in two different ways: natively through the Android SDK (in this chapter) or by using OpenGL ES (in the remaining chapters). Each method requires slightly different ways of storing and treating the images.

The other important tip is that the image names must be all lowercase; this is common with any method of dealing with Android images. If you use capitalization or camel casing in the image names, Android will not recognize the images.

Note   As with everything, there are exceptions, and this is no exception. Image names only need to be lowercase if they are stored within the given Android project structure (i.e. the res folder). If you store your images in a compressed file outside of the Android project structure, and read it using a custom-made file reader, you should be able to get away with casing your file names however you like. This issue, though, is outside the scope of this book.

The five images in this chapter should be kept in the `res/drawable-hdpi` folder because they will be read using common Android SDK methods.

In the next section, you will create the files needed to display your main menu.

Creating the Splash Screen and Main Menu

The main menu of Prison Break consists of a splash screen that fades out to the menu screen. The menu screen contains the Start and Exit buttons.

For Prison Break, both the splash screen and the main menu background will be the same image (see Figure 3-2). This gives the effect that the buttons are fading into the background. It is a nice effect that looks better than a static screen.

PrisonbreakActivity

The first file you work with is `PrisonbreakActivity`. This is the main activity that is created when you created the project. Listing 3-1 shows the code for `PrisonbreakActivity.java`.

Listing 3-1. PrisonbreakActivity.java

```
package com.jfdimarzio;

import android.app.Activity;
import android.content.Context;
import android.content.Intent;
import android.os.Bundle;
import android.os.Handler;
import android.view.WindowManager;

public class PrisonbreakActivity extends Activity {
    /** Called when the activity is first created. */
    @Override
    public void onCreate(Bundle savedInstanceState) {
        PBGameVars.display = ((WindowManager) getSystemService(Context.WINDOW_
SERVICE)).getDefaultDisplay();

            super.onCreate(savedInstanceState);
            /*display the splash screen image*/
            setContentView(R.layout.splashscreen);
            /*start up the splash screen and main menu in a time delayed
thread*/
            PBGameVars.context = this;
            new Handler().postDelayed(new Thread() {
                @Override
                public void run() {
```

```
                    Intent mainMenu = new Intent(PrisonbreakActivity.this,
PBMainMenu.class);

PrisonbreakActivity.this.startActivity(mainMenu);

PrisonbreakActivity.this.finish();

overridePendingTransition(R.layout.fadein,R.layout.fadeout);
                }
        }, PBGameVars.GAME_THREAD_DELAY);
    }
}
```

Looking at the code for PrisonbreakActivity, you can see that it references a few other files. The first is multiple, shared variables in a class called PBGameVars.java. Create a new class in your project with this name and add the following public variables to it. (Please note that you will add to this class several times as you progress through this book.)

```
public static Display display;
public static Context context;
public static final int GAME_THREAD_DELAY = 3000;
public static final int MENU_BUTTON_ALPHA = 0;
public static final boolean HAPTIC_BUTTON_FEEDBACK = true;
```

Next, PrisonbreakActivity referenced a layout located at res/layouts/splashscreen. Listing 3-2 shows the contents of splashscreen.xml.

Listing 3-2. splashscreen.xml

```
<?xml version = "1.0" encoding = "utf-8"?>
<FrameLayout
    xmlns:android = "http://schemas.android.com/apk/res/android"
    android:layout_width = "match_parent"
    android:layout_height = "match_parent">
        <ImageView android:id = "@+id/splashScreenImage"
            android:src = "@drawable/prisonbreaksplash"
            android:layout_width = "match_parent"
            android:layout_height = "match_parent">
        </ImageView>
        <TextView
            android:text = "game by: j.f.dimarzio graphics by: ben eagel"
            android:id = "@+id/creditsText"
            android:layout_gravity = "center_horizontal|bottom"
            android:layout_height = "wrap_content"
            android:layout_width = "wrap_content">
        </TextView>
</FrameLayout>
```

The next file called by PrisonbreakActivity is PBMainMenu.java. We are going to skip this file for a minute and come back to it. First, let's look at two more layouts used in PrisonbreakActivity.java.

Look at the overridePendingTransition() call made in the main activity. This call takes in two transitional layouts. The first layout defines the splash screen fade-in, and the second defines the fade-out to the menu screen. Listing 3-3 and Listing 3-4 contain the code for both the fadein.xml and the fadeout.xml, respectively. While they look the same at first glance, there are some key differences.

The fundamental difference is that on fading in, an acceleration interpolator is used; whereas on fading out, a deceleration interpolator is used.

Listing 3-3. fadein.xml

```
<?xml version="1.0" encoding="utf-8"?>
<alpha xmlns:android="http://schemas.android.com/apk/res/android"
    android:interpolator="@android:anim/accelerate_interpolator"
    android:fromAlpha="0.0"
    android:toAlpha="1.0"
    android:duration="1000" />
```

Listing 3-4. fadeout.xml

```
<?xml version="1.0" encoding="utf-8"?>
<alpha xmlns:android="http://schemas.android.com/apk/res/android"
    android:interpolator = "@android:anim/decelerate_interpolator"
    android:fromAlpha="1.0"
    android:toAlpha="0.0"
    android:duration="1000" />
```

The PrisonbreakActivity displays the splash screen image and then fades that image into the PBMainMenu.java call. Let's take a look at what is in PBMainMenu.java.

PBMainMenu

PBMainMenu controls the starting and exiting of your main game loop; therefore, it needs to display two buttons: the Start button and the Exit button. Listing 3-5 shows the current code for PBMainMenu.java (you will add to this code in the next chapter).

Take notice that PBMainMenu is a new activity and must be defined as such in the AndroidManifest for your project.

Listing 3-5. PBMainMenu.java

```
public static Display display;
public static Context context;
public static final int GAME_THREAD_DELAY = 3000;

package com.jfdimarzio;
```

```java
import android.app.Activity;
import android.content.Intent;
import android.os.Bundle;
import android.view.View;
import android.view.View.OnClickListener;
import android.widget.ImageButton;

public class PBMainMenu extends Activity {
    /** Called when the activity is first created. */
    final PBGameVars engine = new PBGameVars();
    @Override
    public void onCreate(Bundle savedInstanceState) {
        super.onCreate(savedInstanceState);
        setContentView(R.layout.main);
        PBGameVars.context = getApplicationContext();

        /** Set menu button options */
        ImageButton start = (ImageButton)findViewById(R.id.btnStart);
        ImageButton exit = (ImageButton)findViewById(R.id.btnExit);

start.getBackground().setAlpha(PBGameVars.MENU_BUTTON_ALPHA);

start.setHapticFeedbackEnabled(PBGameVars.HAPTIC_BUTTON_FEEDBACK);

exit.getBackground().setAlpha(PBGameVars.MENU_BUTTON_ALPHA);

exit.setHapticFeedbackEnabled(PBGameVars.HAPTIC_BUTTON_FEEDBACK);

        exit.setOnClickListener(new OnClickListener(){
            @Override
            public void onClick(View v) {
                int pid = android.os.Process.myPid();
                android.os.Process.killProcess(pid);
            }
        });
    }

}
```

Like `PrisonbreakActivity`, `PBMainMenu` also makes use of three different layout files. The first is the `main.xml`. This layout defines the main menu screen that the player sees. It contains the Start and Exit buttons. Listing 3-6 shows the `main.xml` layout.

Listing 3-6. main.xml

```xml
<?xml version="1.0" encoding="utf-8"?>
<RelativeLayout xmlns:android="http://schemas.android.com/apk/res/android"
    android:orientation="vertical"
    android:layout_width="match_parent"
    android:layout_height="match_parent"
    >
```

```
<ImageView android:id = "@+id/mainMenuImage"
    android:src = "@drawable/prisonbreaksplash"
    android:layout_width = "match_parent"
    android:layout_height = "match_parent">
</ImageView>
<RelativeLayout
    android:id = "@+id/buttons"
    android:layout_width = "match_parent"
    android:layout_height = "wrap_content"
    android:orientation = "horizontal"
    android:layout_alignParentBottom = "true"
    android:layout_marginBottom = "20dp">
    <ImageButton
        android:id = "@+id/btnStart"
        android:clickable = "true"
        android:layout_alignParentLeft = "true"
        android:layout_width = "wrap_content"
        android:src = "@drawable/startselector"
        android:layout_height = "wrap_content" >
    </ImageButton>
    <ImageButton
        android:id = "@+id/btnExit"
        android:layout_width = "wrap_content"
        android:src = "@drawable/exitselector"
        android:layout_height = "wrap_content"
        android:layout_alignParentRight = "true"
        android:clickable = "true" >
    </ImageButton>
</RelativeLayout>
</RelativeLayout>
```

The PBMainMenu also calls two layout files known as selectors. These files define
what happens when the player selects either the Start button or the Exit button.
For the Prison Break game, you want the visible Start and Exit buttons to be
swapped out for the ones that appear as though the player has crushed them
under his finger. The selector layouts handle the swapping of these images.
Listing 3-7 shows the contents of the exit selector and Listing 3-8 shows the
contents of the start selector.

Listing 3-7. exitselector.xml

```
<?xml version = "1.0" encoding = "utf-8"?>
<selector
    xmlns:android = "http://schemas.android.com/apk/res/android">
    <item android:state_pressed = "true" android:drawable = "@drawable/
exitbtndown" />
    <item android:drawable = "@drawable/exitbtn" />
</selector>
```

Listing 3-8. startselector.xml

```
<?xml version="1.0" encoding="utf-8"?>
<selector
    xmlns:android="http://schemas.android.com/apk/res/android">
    <item android:state_pressed="true" android:drawable="@drawable/
startbtndown" />
    <item android:drawable="@drawable/startbtn" />
</selector>
```

You should now be able to compile and run your code. When you do, you should see a splash screen that fades out to a menu. Touching the Exit button kills the main activity and exits the game. Right now, however, touching the Start button does nothing.

Summary

In this chapter, you added nine code files and five images to your first game project. These files, when put together, created a compelling and professional menu screen. You now have a working splash screen and a basic menu system with two options.

In the next chapter, you add code to the Start button to kick off the main game loop. You will also add the game's background image to the screen.

Chapter 4

Drawing the Background

In the last chapter, you created and finalized the main menu to Prison Break. You should have compiled and run your code on either the Android emulator or an Android-based phone in debug mode, and seen a functioning main menu screen. The Exit button of the main menu is wired to kill the game process. As of right now, however, the Start button is not wired to any code.

In this chapter, you will write the code for the Start button and create the background for Prison Break. To draw the game's background to the screen, you will use calls to OpenGL ES. In the previous chapters, you used Android SDK methods to display graphics like the menu screen and the buttons. Moving forward, you will work in the realm of OpenGL ES.

Let's start by writing the code that is activated by the Start button on the main menu.

Starting the Game

The Start button, located on the main menu, is used by the player to start the game. When starting the game, a new Android Activity that controls all of the games functions is launched. Why is the game launched as yet another new Activity?

The game is launched as another Activity so that you, the game developer, have more flexibility in controlling the way your game is executed. If you want to add to your main menu other functions that are not tied directly to your game—for example, a configurator or tally board—this is a good way to keep your game from getting weighed down with superfluous code.

Listing 4-1 shows the PBMainMenu code that you started writing in Chapter 3. The bolded code has been added to launch the PBGame Activity. Add this code to your PBMainMenu. You will create the PBGame Activity next.

Listing 4-1. PBMainMenu.java

```java
package com.jfdimarzio;

import android.app.Activity;
import android.content.Intent;
import android.os.Bundle;
import android.view.View;
import android.view.View.OnClickListener;
import android.widget.ImageButton;

public class PBMainMenu extends Activity {
    /** Called when the activity is first created. */
    final PBGameVars engine = new PBGameVars();
    @Override
    public void onCreate(Bundle savedInstanceState) {
        super.onCreate(savedInstanceState);
        setContentView(R.layout.main);
        PBGameVars.context = getApplicationContext();

        /** Set menu button options */
        ImageButton start = (ImageButton)findViewById(R.id.btnStart);
        ImageButton exit = (ImageButton)findViewById(R.id.btnExit);

start.getBackground().setAlpha(PBGameVars.MENU_BUTTON_ALPHA);

start.setHapticFeedbackEnabled(PBGameVars.HAPTIC_BUTTON_FEEDBACK);

exit.getBackground().setAlpha(PBGameVars.MENU_BUTTON_ALPHA);

exit.setHapticFeedbackEnabled(PBGameVars.HAPTIC_BUTTON_FEEDBACK);

        start.setOnClickListener(new OnClickListener(){
            @Override
            public void onClick(View v) {
                /** Start Game!!!! */
                Intent game = new Intent(getApplicationContext(),PBGame.class);
                PBMainMenu.this.startActivity(game);
            }
        });

        exit.setOnClickListener(new OnClickListener(){
            @Override
            public void onClick(View v) {
                int pid= android.os.Process.myPid();
                android.os.Process.killProcess(pid);
            }
        });
    }
}
```

Notice that when you click the Start button now, the code is telling PBMainMenu to launch the PBGame Activity. You do not have a PBGame yet. Let's create one.

Create a new Activity named PBGame in your Prison Break project. The PBGame is fairly simple as far as code is concerned. PBGame is going to set the content view of the Activity to the game renderer, and control the onPause and onResume events.

> **Note**   Keep in mind that when I talk about onPause and onResume, these are not game functions; rather they are Android methods that are called when Android pauses or resumes your Activity.

The code in your new PBGame Activity should look like that in Listing 4-2.

Listing 4-2. PBGame.java

```java
package com.jfdimarzio;

import android.app.Activity;
import android.os.Bundle;
import android.view.MotionEvent;

public class PBGame extends Activity {
    final PBGameVars gameEngine = new PBGameVars();
    private PBGameView gameView;

    @Override
    public void onCreate(Bundle savedInstanceState) {
        super.onCreate(savedInstanceState);
        gameView = new PBGameView(this);
        setContentView(gameView);
    }

    @Override
    protected void onResume() {
        super.onResume();
        gameView.onResume();
    }

    @Override
    protected void onPause() {
        super.onPause();
        gameView.onPause();
    }

}
```

Notice that the onCreate() method sets the content view of the Activity to a new instance of PBGameView. PBGameView is a new class that extends GLSurfaceView. The next section of this chapter introduces you to the GLSurfaceView as you create the PBGameView.

Creating the SurfaceView and Renderer

In this section, you will create the SurfaceView and Renderer for your game. PBGameView is a simple Android class that extends the OpenGL GLSurfaceView.

If you have never developed in OpenGL ES before, think of the GLSurfaceView as the canvas on which OpenGL draws your game. The GLSurfaceView is what Android displays to the screen. It cannot act alone, however. The GLSurfaceView needs a corresponding GLSurfaceView Renderer to render the game onto the surface.

Starting with the GLSurfaceView, create a new class named PBGameView, and extend GLSurfaceView, as shown in Listing 4-3.

Listing 4-3. PBGameView.java

```
package com.jfdimarzio;

import android.content.Context;
import android.opengl.GLSurfaceView;

public class PBGameView extends GLSurfaceView {
    private PBGameRenderer renderer;

    public PBGameView(Context context) {
        super(context);

        renderer = new PBGameRenderer();

        this.setRenderer(renderer);

    }
}
```

This is a rather small class. You can see that the purpose of the only constructor in the class is to create an instance of a renderer (PBGameRenderer). There is nothing fancy here, so let's move on to creating the renderer.

> **Note**   Before creating the PBGameRenderer, add the following to your PBGameVars:
> ```
> public static final int GAME_THREAD_FPS_SLEEP = (1000/60);
> ```

Create a new class called PBGameRenderer in your Prison Break project. This class needs to extend GLSurfaceView.Renderer, as shown in Listing 4-4.

Listing 4-4. PBGameRenderer.java

```java
package com.jfdimarzio;

import javax.microedition.khronos.egl.EGLConfig;
import javax.microedition.khronos.opengles.GL10;

import android.opengl.GLSurfaceView.Renderer;

public class PBGameRenderer implements Renderer{
    private long loopStart = 0;
    private long loopEnd = 0;
    private long loopRunTime = 0 ;

    @Override
    public void onDrawFrame(GL10 gl) {
        // TODO Auto-generated method stub
        loopStart = System.currentTimeMillis();
        // TODO Auto-generated method stub
        try {
            if (loopRunTime < PBGameVars.GAME_THREAD_FPS_SLEEP){

Thread.sleep(PBGameVars.GAME_THREAD_FPS_SLEEP - loopRunTime);
            }
        } catch (InterruptedException e) {
            // TODO Auto-generated catch block
            e.printStackTrace();
        }
        gl.glClear(GL10.GL_COLOR_BUFFER_BIT | GL10.GL_DEPTH_BUFFER_BIT);

        loopEnd = System.currentTimeMillis();
        loopRunTime = ((loopEnd - loopStart));
    }

    @Override
    public void onSurfaceChanged(GL10 gl, int width, int height) {
        // TODO Auto-generated method stub
        gl.glViewport(0, 0, width,height);

        gl.glMatrixMode(GL10.GL_PROJECTION);
        gl.glLoadIdentity();

        gl.glOrthof(0f, 1f, 0f, 1f, -1f, 1f);
    }

    @Override
    public void onSurfaceCreated(GL10 gl, EGLConfig arg1) {
        // TODO Auto-generated method stub

        gl.glEnable(GL10.GL_TEXTURE_2D);
        gl.glClearDepthf(1.0f);
```

```
        gl.glEnable(GL10.GL_DEPTH_TEST);
        gl.glDepthFunc(GL10.GL_LEQUAL);

    }
}
```

The renderer has three methods that you need to override: onSurfaceCreated(), onSurfaceChanged(), and onDrawFrame(). As a developer, you will not call any of these methods in your code. The GLSurfaceView is responsible for calling all of these methods at the correct times.

In short, the onSurfaceCreated() acts as the constructor for the renderer and is called when the renderer is created. If everything is running smoothly, this should only be called once; so all of your setup code goes into this method. Right now, the only code that you are calling in your setup routine is OpenGL functions, to set up the texture and depth buffers.

The onSurfaceChanged() method is called whenever the surface is changed. Do not confuse this with onDrawFrame(), however. Drawing a frame does not constitute a surface change. A surface change is more on the lines of a change in screen orientation or a similar destructive event. The onSurfaceChanged() method is also called the first time the renderer is called, after the setup.

In onSurfaceChanged(), you want to set up your game's view port and call OpenGL's rendering pipeline to draw your objects. The game's view port is the area of the game world that is drawn on the screen. Think of the view port as the display on a camera. When you point the camera in a specific direction, you only see a small portion of the entire world. So too, when you create a game using OpenGL: you may create more "objects" in your world than you can see at one time. The view port tells OpenGL what you expect to see rendered to your display.

> **Caution**   Be careful when you are using the width and height variables that are passed into onSurfaceChanged(). When GLSurfaceView calls onSurfaceChanged(), the width and height that are passed in are not necessarily the true width and height of the screen. To get the full width and height of the screen, use the context.display.width and context.display.height.

You want to put all of the code that is called on every frame in the onDrawFrame(). This includes frame-rate calculators, the code for drawing all of the objects in the game, collision detection, and cleanup. The only code that is running on each frame in Listing 4-4 is the thread marshal for the frame rate, as well as an OpenGL method for clearing the buffers.

In the next section, you will create the class that draws the background; and then, you will call that class from the onDrawFrame() and draw the background to the screen.

Creating the Background Class

In Prison Break, you are going to create a class that handles the setup of the indexes, vertices, and textures used to draw the background for your game. Each new element that we add to this game follows the format of this class. The background image that you use should be copied to the res/drawable-nodpi folder in your project and named bg1.png. Add the following variable to your PBGameVars file to help you reference the image later.

```
public static final int BACKGROUND = R.drawable.bg1;
```

The image that I am using is shown in Figure 4-1.

Figure 4-1. bg1.png, the background image for Prison Break

Now it is time to set up the class to create your background. Create a new class in your Prison Break project called PBBackground.java. You need three methods in this class: a constructor, a draw() method, and a loadTexture() method.

The constructor loads up the vertex, index, and texture arrays into buffers. Since this is the most important step in determining what your background looks like when it is rendered to the screen, let's take a little time now to discuss what these arrays are and how they are used.

The vertex array is used to define the corners of the polygon that your background image is mapped to. The corners are defined using their x-, y-, and z-axes on the Cartesian coordinate system. Therefore, in creating a square, you would supply the x-, y-, and z-coordinates of the lower-left corner, upper-left corner, upper-right corner, and lower-right corner, respectively.

Now, I need to clear up some potential confusion in the last paragraph. While in the end, the polygon you draw is a square (or rectangle), OpenGL actually draws in right-angled triangles. Two triangles placed next to each other create a square. The purpose of the index buffer is to tell OpenGL the index order of the triangle's edges, thus telling OpenGL which order the corners in the vertex buffer are drawn. In other words, if the index buffer is 0, 1, 2, 0, 2, 3—like the triangles in Figure 4-2, then the corners in the vertex buffer are the lower-left corner, upper-left corner, upper-right corner, and lower-right corner.

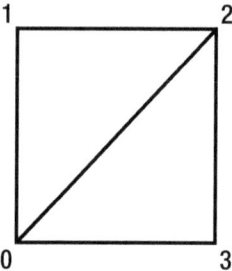

Figure 4-2. Index triangles

Finally, the texture array tells OpenGL which corners of your texture (or image) map to the particular corners of your vertices. Because there is no depth in texture mapping, the texture array only has x- and y-coordinates.

> **Tip**   If you are working with a 3D polygon that has vertices using z-coordinates, and you want to map a texture to the vertices, you still only need to provide the corners of the texture using the x- and y-coordinates. In fact, your texture array will most likely be repeated for every vertex you have. While the vertices will change, if you are working with rectilinear polygons, your texture array will probably stay the same.

The draw() method of the class is called on every frame. This method uses the matrix information that is modified in the renderer to draw the background. It also contains settings for culling the faces of the polygons that are not rendered.

The last method, loadTexture(), contains the calls for taking an image that you pass in, and loading that image into OpenGL as a texture. The class uses this texture in the draw() method. Listing 4-5 shows the code for the PBBackground class.

Listing 4-5. The PBBackground class

```
package com.jfdimarzio;

import java.io.IOException;
import java.io.InputStream;
import java.nio.ByteBuffer;
import java.nio.ByteOrder;
import java.nio.FloatBuffer;

import javax.microedition.khronos.opengles.GL10;

import android.content.Context;
import android.graphics.Bitmap;
import android.graphics.BitmapFactory;
import android.opengl.GLUtils;

public class PBBackground {
    private FloatBuffer vertexBuffer;
    private FloatBuffer textureBuffer;
    private ByteBuffer indexBuffer;

    private int[] textures = new int[1];

    private float vertices[] = {
        0.0f, 0.0f, 0.0f,
        1.0f, 0.0f, 0.0f,
        1.0f, 1.0f, 0.0f,
        0.0f, 1.0f, 0.0f,
    };

    private float texture[] = {
        0.0f, 0.0f,
        1.0f, 0f,
        1f, 1.0f,
        0f, 1f,
    };
```

```
    private byte indices[] = {
        0,1,2,
        0,2,3,
    };

    public PBBackground() {
        ByteBuffer byteBuf = ByteBuffer.allocateDirect(vertices.length * 4);
        byteBuf.order(ByteOrder.nativeOrder());
        vertexBuffer = byteBuf.asFloatBuffer();
        vertexBuffer.put(vertices);
        vertexBuffer.position(0);

        byteBuf = ByteBuffer.allocateDirect(texture.length * 4);
        byteBuf.order(ByteOrder.nativeOrder());
        textureBuffer = byteBuf.asFloatBuffer();
        textureBuffer.put(texture);
        textureBuffer.position(0);
        indexBuffer = ByteBuffer.allocateDirect(indices.length);
        indexBuffer.put(indices);
        indexBuffer.position(0);
    }

    public void draw(GL10 gl) {
        gl.glBindTexture(GL10.GL_TEXTURE_2D, textures[0]);

        gl.glFrontFace(GL10.GL_CCW);
        gl.glEnable(GL10.GL_CULL_FACE);
        gl.glCullFace(GL10.GL_BACK);

        gl.glEnableClientState(GL10.GL_VERTEX_ARRAY);

gl.glEnableClientState(GL10.GL_TEXTURE_COORD_ARRAY);

        gl.glVertexPointer(3, GL10.GL_FLOAT, 0, vertexBuffer);
        gl.glTexCoordPointer(2, GL10.GL_FLOAT, 0, textureBuffer);

        gl.glDrawElements(GL10.GL_TRIANGLES, indices.length, GL10.GL_UNSIGNED_
BYTE, indexBuffer);

        gl.glDisableClientState(GL10.GL_VERTEX_ARRAY);

gl.glDisableClientState(GL10.GL_TEXTURE_COORD_ARRAY);

        gl.glDisable(GL10.GL_CULL_FACE);
    }

    public void loadTexture(GL10 gl,int texture, Context context) {
        InputStream imagestream = context.getResources().
openRawResource(texture);
        Bitmap bitmap = null;
```

```
    try {

        bitmap = BitmapFactory.decodeStream(imagestream);

    }catch(Exception e){

    }finally {
        try {
        imagestream.close();
        imagestream = null;
        } catch (IOException e) {
        }
    }
    gl.glGenTextures(1, textures, 0);
    gl.glBindTexture(GL10.GL_TEXTURE_2D, textures[0]);

    gl.glTexParameterf(GL10.GL_TEXTURE_2D, GL10.GL_TEXTURE_MIN_FILTER,
GL10.GL_NEAREST);
        gl.glTexParameterf(GL10.GL_TEXTURE_2D, GL10.GL_TEXTURE_MAG_FILTER,
GL10.GL_LINEAR);

    GLUtils.texImage2D(GL10.GL_TEXTURE_2D, 0, bitmap, 0);

    bitmap.recycle();
    }
}
```

In the final section of this chapter, you take the PBBackground class and call it from the PBGameRenderer, thus drawing your background to the screen using OpenGL.

Drawing the Background

In this section, you create a new instance of your background and call it from the PBGameRenderer. The steps to draw your background are as follows:

1. Instantiate a new PBBackground. This is pretty self-explanatory; before you can use the background class, you must instantiate it.

2. Load your bg1.png image as the background's texture. Because the image only needs to be loaded once, you call the background class's loadTexture() method in the onSurfaceCreated() method of the PBGameRenderer.

3. Create a new method in PBGameRenderer that adjusts the size of the background's polygons. If you do not adjust the size of the polygons, they will not match the

size that you are expecting them to be on the screen. This step may take some tweaking for you to get just right.

4.   Call this new method from onDrawFrame(). This draws your background to the screen on every frame. If you do not call the method here, it will not render.

Listing 4-6 shows the code for PBGameRenderer; the new code for drawing the background is in bold.

Listing 4-6. PBGameRenderer with Calls to Draw Background

```
package com.jfdimarzio;

import javax.microedition.khronos.egl.EGLConfig;
import javax.microedition.khronos.opengles.GL10;
import android.opengl.GLSurfaceView.Renderer;

public class PBGameRenderer implements Renderer{

    private PBBackground background = new PBBackground();

    private long loopStart = 0;
    private long loopEnd = 0;
    private long loopRunTime = 0 ;

    @Override
    public void onDrawFrame(GL10 gl) {
        // TODO Auto-generated method stub
        loopStart = System.currentTimeMillis();
        // TODO Auto-generated method stub
        try {
            if (loopRunTime < PBGameVars.GAME_THREAD_FPS_SLEEP){

Thread.sleep(PBGameVars.GAME_THREAD_FPS_SLEEP - loopRunTime);
            }
        } catch (InterruptedException e) {
            // TODO Auto-generated catch block
            e.printStackTrace();
        }
        gl.glClear(GL10.GL_COLOR_BUFFER_BIT | GL10.GL_DEPTH_BUFFER_BIT);

        drawBackground1(gl);

        loopEnd = System.currentTimeMillis();
        loopRunTime = ((loopEnd - loopStart));
    }
```

```
    @Override
    public void onSurfaceChanged(GL10 gl, int width, int height) {
        // TODO Auto-generated method stub
        gl.glViewport(0, 0, width,height);

        gl.glMatrixMode(GL10.GL_PROJECTION);
        gl.glLoadIdentity();

        gl.glOrthof(0f, 1f, 0f, 1f, -1f, 1f);
    }

    @Override
    public void onSurfaceCreated(GL10 gl, EGLConfig arg1) {
        // TODO Auto-generated method stub

        gl.glEnable(GL10.GL_TEXTURE_2D);
        gl.glClearDepthf(1.0f);
        gl.glEnable(GL10.GL_DEPTH_TEST);
        gl.glDepthFunc(GL10.GL_LEQUAL);

        background.loadTexture(gl,PBGameVars.BACKGROUND, PBGameVars.context);
    }

    private void drawBackground1(GL10 gl){

        gl.glMatrixMode(GL10.GL_MODELVIEW);
        gl.glLoadIdentity();
        gl.glPushMatrix();
        gl.glScalef(1f, 1f, 1f);

        background.draw(gl);
        gl.glPopMatrix();
    }
}
```

Compile and run your project. At the main menu, click the Start button. You should see the background, as shown in Figure 4-3.

Figure 4-3. The rendered background

Before closing this chapter, let's have a quick word about OpenGL matrix modes. Having seen the call in the PBGameRenderer, you may be confused by what these do. OpenGL has three modes in which you can modify a different matrix in the rendering pipeline. The three modes (and matrices) are ModelView, Texture, and Projection. Working in these modes requires some abstract thinking, but it is not too hard to grasp.

Placing OpenGL into ModelView mode loads the ModelView matrix. The ModelView matrix controls every set of polygons in your OpenGL world.

The Texture mode, on the other hand, loads up the matrix for all of the textures in your world. Keep in mind, while you associate a texture with a set of vertices, in the OpenGL world, they are still contained within two different matrices. The wording here is important. If there are 50 objects on your screen, each with a texture, placing OpenGL in Texture mode gives you access to all 50 textures—not just the one you think you want to work on.

The Project mode loads the matrix that controls OpenGL's camera.

> **Note** OpenGL does not really have or understand the concept of a "camera" as such. Most people understand that a camera is used to create a view and renderer, so it is easy to equate what happens in the Project matrix to the common graphics concept of a camera.

Within each matrix mode, there are specific commands that you can use to work with the objects in those matrices.

The command glLoadIdentity() tells OpenGL to load an unaltered copy of the matrix in question. Let's say, for example, you are in Texture mode and you have a red texture that you mapped to a square. While in Texture mode, you swap the texture for a green one. Calling glLoadIdentity() loads the texture matrix with the red texture.

The command glPushMatrix() performs a similar function. This command gives you a copy of the current matrix, in its current state. Therefore, in our last example, if you were to call glPushMatrix() rather than glLoadIdentity(), you would get a copy of the matrix with a green texture. If you call glPushMatrix() after you call glLoadIdentity(), however, then you would get a copy of the matrix with a red texture.

Once you are done working with the copy of the matrix that you created using glPushMatrix(), use glPopMatrix() to write that copy back to the OpenGL pipeline. This is useful if you have multiple transformations that you want to make on a matrix and you do not want to cause any inadvertent problems to the main matrix.

Finally, there are three commands that you can use to transform your matrices: glScale, glTranslate, and glRotate. As their names imply, glScale and glRotate scale and rotate a matrix, respectively. Again, the effect of these commands depends greatly on the matrix mode you are in. The glTranslate command moves the matrix by the given set of coordinates. These commands are explored in more detail in upcoming chapters.

Summary

In this chapter, you learned how to use OpenGL to create and draw a background to the screen. You also worked with OpenGL Renderers and SurfaceViews. Finally, you created classes that handled the support of OpenGL vertices, textures, and indices.

In the next chapter, you begin to add the blocks and the player's paddle.

Chapter **5**

Creating the Player Character and Obstacles

In the previous chapter, you learned how to add a background image to your game, Prison Break. You created a class that, when instantiated, gave you all of the resources you needed to add your background.

In this chapter, you are going to take that knowledge and apply it to the game's bricks, player paddle, and ball. This will give you all of the on-screen objects you need to make the game.

Before you begin working on the bricks, paddle, or ball, however, there are some things you need to do.

Before You Begin

You need to add a few things to your project to prepare for this chapter, the first being the images that you will use for the bricks, the paddle, and the ball. The image that I used for my bricks (there are a multitude of different bricks that could be used in the game) is a *spritesheet*, which allows you to use different images more easily by containing all of the images for the different bricks in one physical file.

If you have never worked with one, a spritesheet is a single-image file that contains within it all of the different images for a specific animation or set of characters. For example, if you were making a game where the main character could walk across the screen, the spritesheet for that character would contain all of the frames used to make the character animation.

Likewise, to give you—the game developer—some choice in how the game looks, the image for the ball is in a spritesheet as well. This spritesheet has two different ball images for you to choose from.

The images that I used in Prison Break for the brick spritesheet, the player paddle, and the ball spritesheet are shown in Figure 5-1, Figure 5-2, and Figure 5-3, respectively.

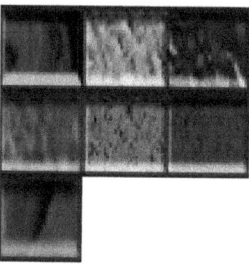

Figure 5-1. The brick spritesheet

Figure 5-2. The player paddle

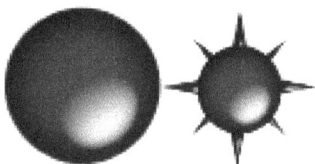

Figure 5-3. The ball spritesheet

You may notice that the bricks and the player paddle are nearly square, rather than rectangular. This is good because it gives you a chance to stretch the image into a rectangle using OpenGL.

Next, you need to add some more variables to the PBGameVars file. Add the following lines to your PBGameVars. Don't worry too much about the ones that you don't understand right now; I will explain them when we use them.

```
public static float playerBankPosX = -.73f;
public static int playerAction = 0;
public static final int PLAYER_MOVE_LEFT_1 = 1;
public static final int PLAYER_RELEASE = 3;
public static final int PLAYER_MOVE_RIGHT_1 = 4;
```

```
public static final float PLAYER_MOVE_SPEED = .2f;
public static final int PADDLE = R.drawable.goldbrick;
public static final int BRICK_BLUE = 1;
public static final int BRICK_BROWN = 2;
public static final int BRICK_DARK_GRAY = 3;
public static final int BRICK_GREEN = 4;
public static final int BRICK_LITE_GRAY = 5;
public static final int BRICK_PURPLE = 6;
public static final int BRICK_RED = 7;
public static final int BRICK_SHEET = R.drawable.bricksheet;
public static final int BALL_SHEET = R.drawable.ballsheet;
public static final float BALL_SPEED = 0.01f;
public static float ballTargetY = 0.01f;
public static float ballTargetX = -1.125f;
```

With this little bit of housekeeping taken care of, it is time to jump into creating some items for the game. Let's start with the player paddle.

Creating the Player Paddle Class

Add a new class called PBPlayer to your project. This class will look very much like the class that you created for the background, PBBackground. The class contains a constructor, a draw() method, and a loadTexture() method. The code for the PBPlayer class is shown in Listing 5-1.

Listing 5-1. The PBPlayer Class

```
package com.jfdimarzio;

import java.io.IOException;
import java.io.InputStream;
import java.nio.ByteBuffer;
import java.nio.ByteOrder;
import java.nio.FloatBuffer;

import javax.microedition.khronos.opengles.GL10;

import android.content.Context;
import android.graphics.Bitmap;
import android.graphics.BitmapFactory;
import android.opengl.GLUtils;

public class PBPlayer {

        private FloatBuffer vertexBuffer;
        private FloatBuffer textureBuffer;
        private ByteBuffer indexBuffer;
```

```java
private int[] textures = new int[1];

private float vertices[] = {
        0.0f, 0.0f, 0.0f,
        1.5f, 0.0f, 0.0f,
        1.5f, .25f, 0.0f,
        0.0f, .25f, 0.0f,
};

private float texture[] = {
        0.0f, 0.0f,
        1.0f, 0.0f,
        1.0f, 1.0f,
        0.0f, 1.0f,
};

private byte indices[] = {
        0,1,2,
        0,2,3,
};

public PBPlayer() {
        ByteBuffer byteBuf = ByteBuffer.allocateDirect(vertices.length * 4);
        byteBuf.order(ByteOrder.nativeOrder());
        vertexBuffer = byteBuf.asFloatBuffer();
        vertexBuffer.put(vertices);
        vertexBuffer.position(0);

        byteBuf = ByteBuffer.allocateDirect(texture.length * 4);
        byteBuf.order(ByteOrder.nativeOrder());
        textureBuffer = byteBuf.asFloatBuffer();
        textureBuffer.put(texture);
        textureBuffer.position(0);

        indexBuffer = ByteBuffer.allocateDirect(indices.length);
        indexBuffer.put(indices);
        indexBuffer.position(0);
}

public void draw(GL10 gl) {
        gl.glBindTexture(GL10.GL_TEXTURE_2D, textures[0]);

        gl.glFrontFace(GL10.GL_CCW);
        gl.glEnable(GL10.GL_CULL_FACE);
        gl.glCullFace(GL10.GL_BACK);

        gl.glEnableClientState(GL10.GL_VERTEX_ARRAY);
        gl.glEnableClientState(GL10.GL_TEXTURE_COORD_ARRAY);
```

```
            gl.glVertexPointer(3, GL10.GL_FLOAT, 0, vertexBuffer);
            gl.glTexCoordPointer(2, GL10.GL_FLOAT, 0, textureBuffer);

            gl.glDrawElements(GL10.GL_TRIANGLES, indices.length, GL10.
GL_UNSIGNED_BYTE, indexBuffer);

            gl.glDisableClientState(GL10.GL_VERTEX_ARRAY);
            gl.glDisableClientState(GL10.GL_TEXTURE_COORD_ARRAY);
            gl.glDisable(GL10.GL_CULL_FACE);
    }

    public void loadTexture(GL10 gl,int texture, Context context) {
            InputStream imagestream=
context.getResources().openRawResource(texture);
            Bitmap bitmap=null;
            try {
                    bitmap=BitmapFactory.decodeStream(imagestream);
            }catch(Exception e){

            }finally {
                    try {
                            imagestream.close();
                            imagestream=null;
                    } catch (IOException e) {
                    }
            }

            gl.glGenTextures(1, textures, 0);
            gl.glBindTexture(GL10.GL_TEXTURE_2D, textures[0]);

            gl.glTexParameterf(GL10.GL_TEXTURE_2D, GL10.GL_TEXTURE_MIN_FILTER,
GL10.GL_NEAREST);
            gl.glTexParameterf(GL10.GL_TEXTURE_2D, GL10.GL_TEXTURE_MAG_FILTER,
GL10.GL_LINEAR);
            GLUtils.texImage2D(GL10.GL_TEXTURE_2D, 0, bitmap, 0);

            bitmap.recycle();
    }
}
```

In the next section, you will add the class for the bricks. Later in the chapter, you add the code that instantiates and calls all of the classes together.

Creating the Brick Class

Just like the player paddle and the background, you need a class that will represent your bricks. The class for the bricks is going to be a little different, however. Because you are going to use a spritesheet with the bricks class, you will not call loadTexture() the same way that you would with the background and the player paddle. Just to give you some perspective on how flexible the code can be, you are going to load all of the spritesheets into an array and pass them together. Therefore, we are going to remove the loadTexture() method and create a new class to handle spritesheet textures.

The code doesn't have to be written this way; rather, because this book is a teaching tool, I am trying to show you different ways to do things. This is simply a good place to take a look at a different way of getting something done. Feel free, after you learn the differences, to use whichever method of texture loading you feel is best for your situation.

First, create a new class called PBBricks. The code for PBBricks is shown in Listing 5-2.

Listing 5-2. PBBrick

```
PBBRick

package com.jfdimarzio;

import java.nio.ByteBuffer;
import java.nio.ByteOrder;
import java.nio.FloatBuffer;

import javax.microedition.khronos.opengles.GL10;

public class PBBrick {

        public float posY = 0f;
        public float posX = 0f;
        public float posT = 0f;

        public boolean isDestroyed = false;

        public int brickType = 0;


        private FloatBuffer vertexBuffer;
        private FloatBuffer textureBuffer;
        private ByteBuffer indexBuffer;

        private float vertices[] = {
                0.0f, 0.0f, 0.0f,
                1.0f, 0.0f, 0.0f,
                1.0f, .25f, 0.0f,
                0.0f, .25f, 0.0f,
        };
```

```
        private float texture[]={
                0.0f, 0.0f,
                0.25f, 0.0f,
                0.25f, 0.25f,
                0.0f, 0.25f,
        };

        private byte indices[]={
                0,1,2,
                0,2,3,
        };

        public PBBrick(int type) {
                brickType=type;
                ByteBuffer byteBuf=ByteBuffer.allocateDirect(vertices.length * 4);
                byteBuf.order(ByteOrder.nativeOrder());
                vertexBuffer=byteBuf.asFloatBuffer();
                vertexBuffer.put(vertices);
                vertexBuffer.position(0);

                byteBuf=ByteBuffer.allocateDirect(texture.length * 4);
                byteBuf.order(ByteOrder.nativeOrder());
                textureBuffer=byteBuf.asFloatBuffer();
                textureBuffer.put(texture);
                textureBuffer.position(0);

                indexBuffer=ByteBuffer.allocateDirect(indices.length);
                indexBuffer.put(indices);
                indexBuffer.position(0);
        }

        public void draw(GL10 gl, int[] spriteSheet) {
                gl.glBindTexture(GL10.GL_TEXTURE_2D, spriteSheet[0]);

                gl.glFrontFace(GL10.GL_CCW);
                gl.glEnable(GL10.GL_CULL_FACE);
                gl.glCullFace(GL10.GL_BACK);
                gl.glEnableClientState(GL10.GL_VERTEX_ARRAY);
                gl.glEnableClientState(GL10.GL_TEXTURE_COORD_ARRAY);

                gl.glVertexPointer(3, GL10.GL_FLOAT, 0, vertexBuffer);
                gl.glTexCoordPointer(2, GL10.GL_FLOAT, 0, textureBuffer);

                gl.glDrawElements(GL10.GL_TRIANGLES, indices.length,
GL10.GL_UNSIGNED_BYTE, indexBuffer);

                gl.glDisableClientState(GL10.GL_VERTEX_ARRAY);
                gl.glDisableClientState(GL10.GL_TEXTURE_COORD_ARRAY);
                gl.glDisable(GL10.GL_CULL_FACE);
        }
}
```

> **Caution**   Pay close attention to the code in bold. It is different from the other
> draw() methods that you have created and it is important for loading the
> correct texture later in the chapter.

Since the PBBrick is using a spritesheet for its texture—as is the PBBall,
which you will create later in the chapter—you need to make a new class
that handles the texture loading for you.

Create a new class called PBTextures. The PBTextures class holds an array of
textures, and serves up the correct one to the proper class that needs it. You
should recognize the code in PBTextures as being from the loadTexture()
method. The code for the PBTexture class is shown in Listing 5-3.

Listing 5-3. PBTextures

```
package com.jfdimarzio;

import java.io.IOException;
import java.io.InputStream;

import javax.microedition.khronos.opengles.GL10;

import android.content.Context;
import android.graphics.Bitmap;
import android.graphics.BitmapFactory;
import android.opengl.GLUtils;

public class PBTextures {

        private int[] textures = new int[3];

        public PBTextures(GL10 gl){

                gl.glGenTextures(3, textures, 0);

        }

        public int[] loadTexture(GL10 gl, int texture, Context context, int
textureNumber) {
```

```
                InputStream imagestream=
context.getResources().openRawResource(texture);
                Bitmap bitmap=null;
                try {
                        bitmap=BitmapFactory.decodeStream(imagestream);
                }catch(Exception e){

                }finally {
                        try {
                                imagestream.close();
                                imagestream=null;
                        } catch (IOException e) {
                        }
                }

                gl.glBindTexture(GL10.GL_TEXTURE_2D, textures[textureNumber - 1]);

                gl.glTexParameterf(GL10.GL_TEXTURE_2D, GL10.GL_TEXTURE_MIN_FILTER,
GL10.GL_NEAREST);
                gl.glTexParameterf(GL10.GL_TEXTURE_2D, GL10.GL_TEXTURE_MAG_FILTER,
GL10.GL_LINEAR);

                gl.glTexParameterf(GL10.GL_TEXTURE_2D, GL10.GL_TEXTURE_WRAP_S,
GL10.GL_CLAMP_TO_EDGE);
                gl.glTexParameterf(GL10.GL_TEXTURE_2D, GL10.GL_TEXTURE_WRAP_T,
GL10.GL_CLAMP_TO_EDGE);

                GLUtils.texImage2D(GL10.GL_TEXTURE_2D, 0, bitmap, 0);

                bitmap.recycle();
                return textures;
        }
}
```

With the PBTextures class out of the way, it is time to create the final object class, PBBall.

Create the PBBall Class

Create a new class called PBBall. This class, like the PBBrick, uses a spritesheet, so no loadTexture() is needed. The PBBall class is very much like the PBBrick. Watch for the code in bold, however; it contains an important change that is necessary for displaying the correct texture later.

The code for the PBBall is shown in Listing 5-4.

Listing 5-4. PBBall

```java
package com.jfdimarzio;

import java.nio.ByteBuffer;
import java.nio.ByteOrder;
import java.nio.FloatBuffer;
import java.util.Random;

import javax.microedition.khronos.opengles.GL10;

public class PBBall {
        public float posY=0f;
        public float posX=0f;
        public float posT=0f;

        public int ballMode=0;

        private Random randomPos=new Random();
        private int damage=0;
        private FloatBuffer vertexBuffer;
        private FloatBuffer textureBuffer;
        private ByteBuffer indexBuffer;

        private float vertices[]={
                0.0f, 0.0f, 0.0f,
                0.25f, 0.0f, 0.0f,
                0.25f, 0.25f, 0.0f,
                0.0f, 0.25f, 0.0f,
        };

        private float texture[]={
                0.0f, 0.0f,
                0.50f, 0.0f,
                0.50f, 0.50f,
                0.0f, 0.50f,
        };

        private byte indices[]={
                0,1,2,
                0,2,3,
        };


        public PBBall() {
                posY=(randomPos.nextFloat()+1f) * (float)(-1.75 - -1.6);
                posX=randomPos.nextFloat() * .75f;
```

```
            ByteBuffer byteBuf=ByteBuffer.allocateDirect(vertices.length * 4);
            byteBuf.order(ByteOrder.nativeOrder());
            vertexBuffer=byteBuf.asFloatBuffer();
            vertexBuffer.put(vertices);
            vertexBuffer.position(0);

            byteBuf=ByteBuffer.allocateDirect(texture.length * 4);
            byteBuf.order(ByteOrder.nativeOrder());
            textureBuffer=byteBuf.asFloatBuffer();
            textureBuffer.put(texture);
            textureBuffer.position(0);

            indexBuffer=ByteBuffer.allocateDirect(indices.length);
            indexBuffer.put(indices);
            indexBuffer.position(0);
        }

}



        public void draw(GL10 gl, int[] spriteSheet) {
                gl.glBindTexture(GL10.GL_TEXTURE_2D, spriteSheet[2]);

                gl.glFrontFace(GL10.GL_CCW);
                gl.glEnable(GL10.GL_CULL_FACE);
                gl.glCullFace(GL10.GL_BACK);

                gl.glEnableClientState(GL10.GL_VERTEX_ARRAY);
                gl.glEnableClientState(GL10.GL_TEXTURE_COORD_ARRAY);

                gl.glVertexPointer(3, GL10.GL_FLOAT, 0, vertexBuffer);
                gl.glTexCoordPointer(2, GL10.GL_FLOAT, 0, textureBuffer);

                gl.glDrawElements(GL10.GL_TRIANGLES, indices.length,
GL10.GL_UNSIGNED_BYTE, indexBuffer);

                gl.glDisableClientState(GL10.GL_VERTEX_ARRAY);
                gl.glDisableClientState(GL10.GL_TEXTURE_COORD_ARRAY);
                gl.glDisable(GL10.GL_CULL_FACE);
        }
}
```

Now that you have all of your classes ready for your bricks, paddle, and ball, it is time to put them together and learn how to call them in the PBGameRenderer, right? Not quite. There are two smaller helper classes that you are going to need just to make life easier later on.

The PBRow and the PBWall

Undoubtedly, you have seen a *Breakout*-style game in the past. In these games, the bricks that you must break through are arranged in a brick wall pattern. This, too, is the case in Prison Break.

You are going to create two classes, PBRow and PBWall, to help make the task of instantiating multiple bricks and laying them out in a brick wall–style pattern. The PBWall class is going to be made up of a specified number of rows. These rows are separate instances of PBRow, which in turn is made of a predetermined number and layout of PBBrick. Therefore, when you initialize your game, you will only need to create an instance of PBWall and tell it how many rows you would like; PBWall will take care of the rest.

Create a new class called PBWall. The code for PBWall is shown in Listing 5-5-

Listing 5-5. PBWall

```java
package com.jfdimarzio;

public class PBWall {
        public PBRow[] rows;

        public PBWall(int numberOfRows){

                rows = new PBRow[numberOfRows];

                for(int x = 0; x <= numberOfRows - 1; x ++)
                {
                        rows[x] = new PBRow(x);
                }
        }
}
```

Next, create a new class called PBRow in your project. The code for PBRow is shown in Listing 5-6.

Listing 5-6. PBRow

```java
package com.jfdimarzio;

import java.util.Random;

public class PBRow {
        public PBBrick[] bricks;
        private Random brickType = new Random();
        private boolean isRowOdd = false;
```

```
    private int numberOfBricks=0;

        public PBRow(int rowNumber){

        if(rowNumber          2>0)
        {
                numberOfBricks=4;
                isRowOdd=true;
        }
        else
        {
                numberOfBricks=5;
                isRowOdd=false;
        }

        bricks=new PBBrick[numberOfBricks];

        for(int x=0; x<numberOfBricks ; x++)
        {
                bricks[x]=new PBBrick((int) (brickType.nextFloat() * 7));
                if(isRowOdd)
                {
                        bricks[x].posX=x - 2f ;
                        bricks[x].posY=(rowNumber * .25f)+1 ;
                }
                else
                {
                        bricks[x].posX=x - 2.5f;
                        bricks[x].posY=(rowNumber * .25f)+1 ;
                }
        }
    }
}
```

I bolded one piece of code from PBRow to pay special attention to. This line creates a random number and assigns it to the brickType. Later in the PBGameRenderer, you will use this random brickType to determine the color (and texture) of the brick.

Now we put everything together in the PBGameRenderer.

Calling the Bricks, Paddle, and Ball in the PBGameRenderer

In this section of the chapter, I highlight the code that you need to add to the PBGameRenderer. After I highlight the code, I will give you the full code for the PBGameRenderer class so that you can see it in context.

The first thing you will need to do is create variables for your wall, paddle, ball, spritesheets, and so on. The following are the new variables you will need to add to the PBGameRenderer:

```
private PBPlayer player1 = new PBPlayer();
private PBBall ball = new PBBall();
private PBTextures textureLoader;
private int[] spriteSheets = new int[3];
private int numberOfRows = 4;
private PBWall wall;
```

With the variables in place, you need to add some texture loaders to the onSurfaceCreated() method. The code you need to add is bolded in the following snippet:

```
@Override
public void onSurfaceCreated(GL10 gl, EGLConfig arg1) {
        // TODO Auto-generated method stub
    initializeBricks();
    textureLoader=new PBTextures(gl);
    spriteSheets=textureLoader.loadTexture(gl, PBGameVars.BRICK_SHEET,
PBGameVars.context, 1);

                gl.glEnable(GL10.GL_TEXTURE_2D);
                gl.glClearDepthf(1.0f);
                gl.glEnable(GL10.GL_DEPTH_TEST);
                gl.glDepthFunc(GL10.GL_LEQUAL);

                background.loadTexture(gl,PBGameVars.BACKGROUND, PBGameVars.
context);
player1.loadTexture(gl,PBGameVars.PADDLE, PBGameVars.context);
    }
```

Notice that the onSurfaceCreated() calls a new method, initializeBricks(). This new method creates your wall for you.

```
    private void initializeBricks(){
            wall=new PBWall(numberOfRows);
    }
```

Now you need a method that draws the bricks on each frame; something that can be called in the drawFrame() method, much like the drawBrackground() method. A drawBricks() method calls on every frame and serves a couple of functions. First, by iterating through the PBWall and reading the isDestroyed flag of each brick, it determines whether a brick has been knocked out of the game. If a brick has been destroyed, it is skipped in the drawing loop, thus preventing it from being rendered to the screen, and causing it to disappear from the game.

Second, the drawBricks() method uses a case statement built around the brickType of each brick to determine which of the images in the brick spritesheet to use as a texture for that specific brick. This is an important part of the code to pay attention to because it uses glTranslatef() to move the spritesheet to the correct texture on each brick.

Think of it like this: the brick that is drawn in the game is the size of one brick, but the spritesheet that holds all of the images is the size of seven bricks. Therefore, using glTranslatef(), you are going to move the spritesheet around on the brick until the correct brick image is mapped to the correct brick.

You see this in action in the code that is bolded, as follows:

```
        private void drawBricks(GL10 gl){
                for (int x=0; x<wall.rows.length; x++)
                {
                        for(int y=0; y<wall.rows[x].bricks.length; y++)
                        {
                                if(!wall.rows[x].bricks[y].isDestroyed)
                                {
                                        switch (wall.rows[x].bricks[y].
brickType){
                                                case PBGameVars.BRICK_BLUE:
                                                gl.glMatrixMode(GL10.
GL_MODELVIEW);
                                                gl.glLoadIdentity();
                                                gl.glPushMatrix();
                                                gl.glScalef(.25f, .25f,
1f);
                                                gl.glTranslatef(wall.
rows[x].bricks[y].posX, wall.rows[x].bricks[y].posY, 0f);

gl.glMatrixMode(GL10.GL_TEXTURE);
                                        gl.glLoadIdentity();
                                        gl.glTranslatef(0.50f, 0.25f , 0.0f);
                                        wall.rows[x].bricks[y].draw(gl, spriteSheets);
```

```
                                gl.glPopMatrix();
                                gl.glLoadIdentity();

                                                break;
                                       case PBGameVars.BRICK_BROWN:
gl.glMatrixMode(GL10.GL_MODELVIEW);
                                                gl.glLoadIdentity();
                                                gl.glPushMatrix();
                                                gl.glScalef(.25f, .25f,
1f);
gl.glTranslatef(wall.rows[x].bricks[y].posX, wall.rows[x].bricks[y].posY, 0f);

gl.glMatrixMode(GL10.GL_TEXTURE);
                                                gl.glLoadIdentity();
                                                gl.glTranslatef(0.0f,
0.50f , 0.0f);
                                                wall.rows[x].bricks[y].
draw(gl, spriteSheets);
                                                gl.glPopMatrix();
                                                gl.glLoadIdentity();
                                                break;
                                       case PBGameVars.BRICK_DARK_GRAY:
gl.glMatrixMode(GL10.GL_MODELVIEW);
                                                gl.glLoadIdentity();
                                                gl.glPushMatrix();
                                                gl.glScalef(.25f, .25f,
1f);

gl.glTranslatef(wall.rows[x].bricks[y].posX, wall.rows[x].bricks[y].posY, 0f);

gl.glMatrixMode(GL10.GL_TEXTURE);
                                                gl.glLoadIdentity();
                                                gl.glTranslatef(0.25f,
0.25f , 0.0f);
                                                wall.rows[x].bricks[y].
draw(gl, spriteSheets);
                                                gl.glPopMatrix();
                                                gl.glLoadIdentity();
                                                break;
                                       case PBGameVars.BRICK_GREEN:

gl.glMatrixMode(GL10.GL_MODELVIEW);
                                                gl.glLoadIdentity();
                                                gl.glPushMatrix();
                                                gl.glScalef(.25f, .25f,
1f);
```

```
gl.glTranslatef(wall.rows[x].bricks[y].posX, wall.rows[x].bricks[y].posY, 0f);

gl.glMatrixMode(GL10.GL_TEXTURE);
                                        gl.glLoadIdentity();
                                        gl.glTranslatef(0.0f,
0.25f , 0.0f);
                                        wall.rows[x].bricks[y].
draw(gl, spriteSheets);
                                        gl.glPopMatrix();
                                        gl.glLoadIdentity();
                                        break;
                            case PBGameVars.BRICK_LITE_GRAY:

gl.glMatrixMode(GL10.GL_MODELVIEW);
                                        gl.glLoadIdentity();
                                        gl.glPushMatrix();
                                        gl.glScalef(.25f, .25f,
1f);

gl.glTranslatef(wall.rows[x].bricks[y].posX, wall.rows[x].bricks[y].posY, 0f);

gl.glMatrixMode(GL10.GL_TEXTURE);
                                        gl.glLoadIdentity();
                                        gl.glTranslatef(0.25f,
0.0f , 0.0f);
                                        wall.rows[x].bricks[y].
draw(gl, spriteSheets);
                                        gl.glPopMatrix();
                                        gl.glLoadIdentity();
                                        break;
                            case PBGameVars.BRICK_PURPLE:

gl.glMatrixMode(GL10.GL_MODELVIEW);
                                        gl.glLoadIdentity();
                                        gl.glPushMatrix();
                                        gl.glScalef(.25f, .25f,
1f);

gl.glTranslatef(wall.rows[x].bricks[y].posX, wall.rows[x].bricks[y].posY, 0f);

gl.glMatrixMode(GL10.GL_TEXTURE);
                                        gl.glLoadIdentity();
                                        gl.glTranslatef(0.50f,
0.0f , 0.0f);
                                        wall.rows[x].bricks[y].
draw(gl, spriteSheets);
```

```
                                        gl.glPopMatrix();
                                        gl.glLoadIdentity();
                                        break;
                             case PBGameVars.BRICK_RED:

gl.glMatrixMode(GL10.GL_MODELVIEW);
                                        gl.glLoadIdentity();
                                        gl.glPushMatrix();
                                        gl.glScalef(.25f, .25f,
1f);
gl.glTranslatef(wall.rows[x].bricks[y].posX, wall.rows[x].bricks[y].posY, 0f);

gl.glMatrixMode(GL10.GL_TEXTURE);
                                        gl.glLoadIdentity();
                                        gl.glTranslatef(0.0f,
0.0f , 0.0f);
                                        wall.rows[x].bricks[y].
draw(gl, spriteSheets);
                                        gl.glPopMatrix();
                                        gl.glLoadIdentity();
                                        break;
                             default:

gl.glMatrixMode(GL10.GL_MODELVIEW);
                                        gl.glLoadIdentity();
                                        gl.glPushMatrix();
                                        gl.glScalef(.25f, .25f,
1f);

gl.glTranslatef(wall.rows[x].bricks[y].posX, wall.rows[x].bricks[y].posY, 0f);

gl.glMatrixMode(GL10.GL_TEXTURE);
                                        gl.glLoadIdentity();
                                        gl.glTranslatef(0.0f,
0.0f , 0.0f);
                                        wall.rows[x].bricks[y].
draw(gl, spriteSheets);
                                        gl.glPopMatrix();
                                        gl.glLoadIdentity();
                                        break;
                                }
                            }
                        }
                    }
                }
```

Caution   Keep a close eye on each case in the switch statement. While they may look the same, there is an important difference. Notice the glTranslatef() call of each case in the Texture mode. Each one moves to a different set of coordinates, signifying the different brick images in the spritesheet.

Finally, you need two methods for moving the player paddle and the ball with each new frame. First, in the moveBall() method you will notice that there is some basic trajectory math being performed in the background, just to move it from its random starting point to a point off the screen. This math does not take into account any collision detection or angular deflections; that is covered in the next chapter.

```
        private void moveBall(GL10 gl){
                gl.glMatrixMode(GL10.GL_MODELVIEW);
                gl.glLoadIdentity();
                gl.glPushMatrix();
                gl.glScalef(.25f, .25f, 1f);

                ball.posX+= (float) ((PBGameVars.ballTargetX - ball.posX )/
(ball.posY / (PBGameVars.ballTargetY )));

                ball.posY -=PBGameVars.ballTargetY * 3;

                gl.glTranslatef(ball.posX, ball.posY, 0f);
                gl.glMatrixMode(GL10.GL_TEXTURE);
                gl.glLoadIdentity();
                gl.glTranslatef(0.0f,0.0f, 0.0f);
                ball.draw(gl,spriteSheets);
                gl.glPopMatrix();
                gl.glLoadIdentity();
        }
```

The move paddle is similar; however, it uses some variables from the PBGameVars to determine where to move the player.

```
        private void movePlayer1(GL10 gl){
                gl.glMatrixMode(GL10.GL_MODELVIEW);
                gl.glLoadIdentity();
                gl.glPushMatrix();
                gl.glScalef(.25f, .25f, 1f);

                if (PBGameVars.playerAction == PBGameVars.PLAYER_MOVE_LEFT_1 &&
PBGameVars.playerBankPosX>0)
                {
                        PBGameVars.playerBankPosX=PBGameVars.playerBankPosX -
PBGameVars.PLAYER_MOVE_SPEED;
                }
```

```
                    else if(PBGameVars.playerAction == PBGameVars.PLAYER_MOVE_
RIGHT_1 && PBGameVars.playerBankPosX < 2.5)
                    {
                            PBGameVars.playerBankPosX = PBGameVars.playerBankPosX +
PBGameVars.PLAYER_MOVE_SPEED;
                    }
                    gl.glTranslatef(PBGameVars.playerBankPosX, .5f, 0f);
                    gl.glMatrixMode(GL10.GL_TEXTURE);
                    gl.glLoadIdentity();
                    gl.glTranslatef(0.0f,0.0f, 0.0f);
                    player1.draw(gl);
                    gl.glPopMatrix();
                    gl.glLoadIdentity();
            }
```

The playerAction variable in the previous code sample determines if the player
wants to move the paddle to the left or to the right. In the real world, the player
is touching either to the left or to the right side of the device's screen to move
the paddle. To detect the screen touches and set the appropriate variable, add
the following bolded code to the PBGame file:

```
package com.jfdimarzio;


import android.app.Activity;
import android.os.Bundle;
import android.view.MotionEvent;



public class PBGame extends Activity {
        final PBGameVars gameEngine = new PBGameVars();
        private PBGameView gameView;


        @Override
        public void onCreate(Bundle savedInstanceState) {
                super.onCreate(savedInstanceState);
                gameView = new PBGameView(this);
                setContentView(gameView);
        }


        @Override
        protected void onResume() {
                super.onResume();
                gameView.onResume();
        }
```

```
        @Override
        protected void onPause() {
                super.onPause();
                gameView.onPause();
        }


        @Override
        public boolean onTouchEvent(MotionEvent event) {
            float x = event.getX();
            float y = event.getY();
            int height = PBGameVars.display.getHeight() / 4;
            int playableArea = PBGameVars.display.getHeight() - height;
            if (y > playableArea){
                    switch (event.getAction()){
                        case MotionEvent.ACTION_DOWN:
                            if(x < PBGameVars.display.getWidth() / 2){
                                    PBGameVars.playerAction = PBGameVars.PLAYER_
MOVE_LEFT_1;
                            }else{
                                    PBGameVars.playerAction = PBGameVars.PLAYER_
MOVE_RIGHT_1;
                            }
                            break;
                        case MotionEvent.ACTION_UP:
                            PBGameVars.playerAction = PBGameVars.PLAYER_RELEASE;
                            break;
                    }
            }
            return false;
        }
}
```

The complete PBGameRenderer (as of this chapter) should appear as shown in Listing 5-7. The code that you added in this chapter is in bold.

Listing 5-7. PBGameRenderer

```
package com.jfdimarzio;

import javax.microedition.khronos.egl.EGLConfig;
import javax.microedition.khronos.opengles.GL10;

import android.opengl.GLSurfaceView.Renderer;

public class PBGameRenderer implements Renderer{

        private PBBackground background = new PBBackground();
    private PBPlayer player1 = new PBPlayer();
    private PBBall ball = new PBBall();
```

```java
    private PBTextures textureLoader;
    private int[] spriteSheets = new int[3];
    private int numberOfRows = 4;
    private PBWall wall;

        private long loopStart = 0;
        private long loopEnd = 0;
        private long loopRunTime = 0 ;

        private float bgScroll1;

        @Override
        public void onDrawFrame(GL10 gl) {
                // TODO Auto-generated method stub
                loopStart = System.currentTimeMillis();
                // TODO Auto-generated method stub
                try {
                        if (loopRunTime < PBGameVars.GAME_THREAD_FPS_SLEEP){
                                Thread.sleep(PBGameVars.GAME_THREAD_FPS_SLEEP -
loopRunTime);
                        }
                } catch (InterruptedException e) {
                        // TODO Auto-generated catch block
                        e.printStackTrace();
                }
                gl.glClear(GL10.GL_COLOR_BUFFER_BIT | GL10.GL_DEPTH_BUFFER_BIT);

                drawBackground1(gl);
    movePlayer1(gl);
    drawBricks(gl);
    moveBall(gl);
                loopEnd = System.currentTimeMillis();
                loopRunTime = ((loopEnd - loopStart));
        }

        @Override
        public void onSurfaceChanged(GL10 gl, int width, int height) {
                // TODO Auto-generated method stub
                gl.glViewport(0, 0, width,height);

                gl.glMatrixMode(GL10.GL_PROJECTION);
                gl.glLoadIdentity();

                gl.glOrthof(0f, 1f, 0f, 1f, -1f, 1f);
        }

        @Override
        public void onSurfaceCreated(GL10 gl, EGLConfig arg1) {
                // TODO Auto-generated method stub
```

```java
        initializeBricks();
        textureLoader = new PBTextures(gl);
        spriteSheets = textureLoader.loadTexture(gl, PBGameVars.BRICK_SHEET,
PBGameVars.context, 1);

                gl.glEnable(GL10.GL_TEXTURE_2D);
                gl.glClearDepthf(1.0f);
                gl.glEnable(GL10.GL_DEPTH_TEST);
                gl.glDepthFunc(GL10.GL_LEQUAL);

                background.loadTexture(gl,PBGameVars.BACKGROUND, PBGameVars.
context);
                player1.loadTexture(gl,PBGameVars.PADDLE, PBGameVars.context);
        }

        private void drawBackground1(GL10 gl){

                gl.glMatrixMode(GL10.GL_MODELVIEW);
                gl.glLoadIdentity();
                gl.glPushMatrix();
                gl.glScalef(1f, 1f, 1f);

                background.draw(gl);
                gl.glPopMatrix();
                gl.glLoadIdentity();

        }

    private void initializeBricks(){
        wall = new PBWall(numberOfRows);
    }

    private void drawBricks(GL10 gl){
        for (int x = 0; x < wall.rows.length; x++)
        {
            for(int y = 0; y < wall.rows[x].bricks.length; y++)
            {
                if(!wall.rows[x].bricks[y].isDestroyed)
                {
                    switch (wall.rows[x].bricks[y].brickType){
                        case PBGameVars.BRICK_BLUE:
                            gl.glMatrixMode(GL10.GL_MODELVIEW);
                            gl.glLoadIdentity();
                            gl.glPushMatrix();
                            gl.glScalef(.25f, .25f, 1f);
                            gl.glTranslatef(wall.rows[x].bricks[y].posX,
wall.rows[x].bricks[y].posY, 0f);

                            gl.glMatrixMode(GL10.GL_TEXTURE);
                            gl.glLoadIdentity();
```

```
                                      gl.glTranslatef(0.50f, 0.25f, 0.0f);
                                      wall.rows[x].bricks[y].draw(gl, spriteSheets);
                                      gl.glPopMatrix();
                                      gl.glLoadIdentity();
                                      break;
                          case PBGameVars.BRICK_BROWN:
                                      gl.glMatrixMode(GL10.GL_MODELVIEW);
                                      gl.glLoadIdentity();
                                      gl.glPushMatrix();
                                      gl.glScalef(.25f, .25f, 1f);
                                      gl.glTranslatef(wall.rows[x].bricks[y].posX,
wall.rows[x].bricks[y].posY, 0f);

                                      gl.glMatrixMode(GL10.GL_TEXTURE);
                                      gl.glLoadIdentity();
                                      gl.glTranslatef(0.0f, 0.50f, 0.0f);
                                      wall.rows[x].bricks[y].draw(gl, spriteSheets);
                                      gl.glPopMatrix();
                                      gl.glLoadIdentity();
                                      break;
                          case PBGameVars.BRICK_DARK_GRAY:
                                      gl.glMatrixMode(GL10.GL_MODELVIEW);
                                      gl.glLoadIdentity();
                                      gl.glPushMatrix();
                                      gl.glScalef(.25f, .25f, 1f);
                                      gl.glTranslatef(wall.rows[x].bricks[y].posX,
wall.rows[x].bricks[y].posY, 0f);

                                      gl.glMatrixMode(GL10.GL_TEXTURE);
                                      gl.glLoadIdentity();
                                      gl.glTranslatef(0.25f, 0.25f, 0.0f);
                                      wall.rows[x].bricks[y].draw(gl, spriteSheets);
                                      gl.glPopMatrix();
                                      gl.glLoadIdentity();
                                      break;
                          case PBGameVars.BRICK_GREEN:
                                      gl.glMatrixMode(GL10.GL_MODELVIEW);
                                      gl.glLoadIdentity();
                                      gl.glPushMatrix();
                                      gl.glScalef(.25f, .25f, 1f);
                                      gl.glTranslatef(wall.rows[x].bricks[y].posX,
wall.rows[x].bricks[y].posY, 0f);

                                      gl.glMatrixMode(GL10.GL_TEXTURE);
                                      gl.glLoadIdentity();
                                      gl.glTranslatef(0.0f, 0.25f, 0.0f);
                                      wall.rows[x].bricks[y].draw(gl, spriteSheets);
                                      gl.glPopMatrix();
                                      gl.glLoadIdentity();
                                      break;
                          case PBGameVars.BRICK_LITE_GRAY:
                                      gl.glMatrixMode(GL10.GL_MODELVIEW);
```

```
                                gl.glLoadIdentity();
                                gl.glPushMatrix();
                                gl.glScalef(.25f, .25f, 1f);
                                gl.glTranslatef(wall.rows[x].bricks[y].posX,
wall.rows[x].bricks[y].posY, 0f);

                                gl.glMatrixMode(GL10.GL_TEXTURE);
                                gl.glLoadIdentity();
                                gl.glTranslatef(0.25f, 0.0f, 0.0f);
                                wall.rows[x].bricks[y].draw(gl, spriteSheets);
                                gl.glPopMatrix();
                                gl.glLoadIdentity();
                                break;
                        case PBGameVars.BRICK_PURPLE:
                                gl.glMatrixMode(GL10.GL_MODELVIEW);
                                gl.glLoadIdentity();
                                gl.glPushMatrix();
                                gl.glScalef(.25f, .25f, 1f);
                                gl.glTranslatef(wall.rows[x].bricks[y].posX,
wall.rows[x].bricks[y].posY, 0f);

                                gl.glMatrixMode(GL10.GL_TEXTURE);
                                gl.glLoadIdentity();
                                gl.glTranslatef(0.50f, 0.0f, 0.0f);
                                wall.rows[x].bricks[y].draw(gl, spriteSheets);
                                gl.glPopMatrix();
                                gl.glLoadIdentity();
                                break;
                        case PBGameVars.BRICK_RED:
                                gl.glMatrixMode(GL10.GL_MODELVIEW);
                                gl.glLoadIdentity();
                                gl.glPushMatrix();
                                gl.glScalef(.25f, .25f, 1f);
                                gl.glTranslatef(wall.rows[x].bricks[y].posX,
wall.rows[x].bricks[y].posY, 0f);

                                gl.glMatrixMode(GL10.GL_TEXTURE);
                                gl.glLoadIdentity();
                                gl.glTranslatef(0.0f, 0.0f, 0.0f);
                                wall.rows[x].bricks[y].draw(gl, spriteSheets);
                                gl.glPopMatrix();
                                gl.glLoadIdentity();
                                break;
                    default:
                                gl.glMatrixMode(GL10.GL_MODELVIEW);
                                gl.glLoadIdentity();
                                gl.glPushMatrix();
                                gl.glScalef(.25f, .25f, 1f);
                                gl.glTranslatef(wall.rows[x].bricks[y].posX,
wall.rows[x].bricks[y].posY, 0f);

                                gl.glMatrixMode(GL10.GL_TEXTURE);
                                gl.glLoadIdentity();
```

```
                                gl.glTranslatef(0.0f, 0.0f, 0.0f);
                                wall.rows[x].bricks[y].draw(gl, spriteSheets);
                                gl.glPopMatrix();
                                gl.glLoadIdentity();
                                break;
                    }
                }
            }
        }
    }

    private void moveBall(GL10 gl){
        gl.glMatrixMode(GL10.GL_MODELVIEW);
        gl.glLoadIdentity();
        gl.glPushMatrix();
        gl.glScalef(.25f, .25f, 1f);

        ball.posX += (float) ((PBGameVars.ballTargetX - ball.posX )/ (ball.posY
/(PBGameVars.ballTargetY )));

        ball.posY -= PBGameVars.ballTargetY * 3;

        gl.glTranslatef(ball.posX, ball.posY, 0f);
        gl.glMatrixMode(GL10.GL_TEXTURE);
        gl.glLoadIdentity();
        gl.glTranslatef(0.0f,0.0f, 0.0f);
        ball.draw(gl,spriteSheets);
        gl.glPopMatrix();
        gl.glLoadIdentity();
    }

    private void movePlayer1(GL10 gl){
        gl.glMatrixMode(GL10.GL_MODELVIEW);
        gl.glLoadIdentity();
        gl.glPushMatrix();
        gl.glScalef(.25f, .25f, 1f);

        if (PBGameVars.playerAction == PBGameVars.PLAYER_MOVE_LEFT_1 &&
PBGameVars.playerBankPosX > 0)
    {
            PBGameVars.playerBankPosX = PBGameVars.playerBankPosX -
PBGameVars.PLAYER_MOVE_SPEED;
    }
        else if(PBGameVars.playerAction == PBGameVars.PLAYER_MOVE_RIGHT_1 &&
PBGameVars.playerBankPosX < 2.5)
    {
            PBGameVars.playerBankPosX = PBGameVars.playerBankPosX +
PBGameVars.PLAYER_MOVE_SPEED;
    }
```

```
      gl.glTranslatef(PBGameVars.playerBankPosX, .5f, 0f);
      gl.glMatrixMode(GL10.GL_TEXTURE);
      gl.glLoadIdentity();
      gl.glTranslatef(0.0f,0.0f, 0.0f);
      player1.draw(gl);
      gl.glPopMatrix();
      gl.glLoadIdentity();
   }
}
```

Compile and run your game in the emulator or on your device. You will now see a wall of bricks to destroy, a responsive player paddle, and a ball that quickly moves off the screen.

Summary

In this chapter, you created a wall of randomly colored bricks, a movable player paddle, and a ball. This is a lot of code to add to the game, and it brings you very close to completing the Prison Break game. You also learned how to use a spritesheet, and you created a great helper class that builds a wall of bricks with a specified number of rows.

The ability to use helper classes to do some of the more tedious setup work in a game is a valuable skill that you find yourself using more and more. Try to look for places where you can use helper classes to handle character or object setup in your games.

In the next chapter, you will create the collision detection logic that finishes the playable physics of the game.

Chapter **6**

Collision Detection

In the last chapter, you added all of the game elements to the game world: bricks, a player paddle, and the ball. After running your code, however, you found that although you could move the player paddle, it had no effect on the gameplay. The ball starts in a random position and ends up falling off the bottom of the screen. The reason for this is the distinct lack of collision detection in your game.

In this chapter, you will add collision detection to the game.

The Purpose of Collision Detection

The strict definition of collision detection is, well, detecting when elements on the screen have collided. It is much more crucial than that, however. A good collision detection system tests for and evaluates when elements in the game world come into contact with one another. It also provides you with a method by which to react to those collisions.

The collision detection system for Prison Break is going to be basic, but it will show you how collision detection works and it will allow you to expand upon it as you see fit.

Keep in mind, OpenGL does not have any built-in collision detection or vertex testing capabilities; it just isn't built for that. It is your responsibility as a game developer to provide that mechanism to the game.

Collision Detection in Prison Break

Before we begin to write the collision detection system for Prison Break, we need to discuss what it needs to do. It is always best to have a good idea of how you want a system to work before you begin to code it.

The following is a list of the items that we need to test in the collision detection system for Prison Break:

- Has the ball hit the paddle?
- Has the ball hit a brick?
- Has the ball hit the right "wall" or edge of the screen?
- Has the ball hit the left "wall" or edge of the screen?
- Has the ball exited the upper boundary of the game?
- Has the ball exited the lower boundary of the game?

In addition to these tests, the collision detection system has to perform the following actions:

- "Destroy" any brick that is hit by the ball.
- Calculate the angle of deflection and move the ball along if it hits the paddle or the right or left edges of the game screen.

While this seems like a lot, this is a surprisingly basic collision detection system for your game. Some collision detection systems are incredibly complex.

Creating the Collision Detection System

You will not need to create a new class for the collision detection system; rather, it will reside in a method of the PBGameRenderer. It is important that the collision detection system run on every frame of the game renderer. Therefore, the method will be called from the onDrawFrame().

Create a new method in your PBGameRenderer called detectCollisions(). Let's take a step-by-step look at the code in detectCollisions(). Then I will give you the full code of the PBGameRenderer so that you can see it in context.

The first thing the method does is test to see if the ball is off the bottom edge of the screen. If it is, this indicates a game-over scenario. To determine if the ball is off the edge of the screen, simply test its y-axis position to see if it is less than 0.

```
if(ball.posY <= 0){
//GameOver

}
```

> **Note** When you are testing the x- or y-coordinate positions of anything on the screen in Prison Break, the coordinate given represents the position of the upper left-hand corner of the vertex that the texture is mapped on to. This is important to note because you may need to take into account the width or height of the vertex when testing certain collisions.

Next, you test each brick to see whether or not the ball has contacted it.

```
for (int x=0; x<wall.rows.length; x++)
{
        for(int y=0; y<wall.rows[x].bricks.length; y++)
        {
                if(!wall.rows[x].bricks[y].isDestroyed)
                {
                        if (((ball.posY>wall.rows[x].bricks[y].
                        posY-.25f)
                        && (ball.posY<wall.rows[x].bricks[y].posY)
                        && (ball.posX+.25f>wall.rows[x].bricks[y].posX)
                        && (ball.posX<wall.rows[x].bricks[y].
                        posX+1.50f)))
                        {
                                wall.rows[x].bricks[y].isDestroyed=true;
                                PBGameVars.ballTargetY=PBGameVars.
                                ballTargetY * -1f;
                                if(PBGameVars.ballTargetX == -2f){
                                        PBGameVars.ballTargetX=5f;
                                }else{
                                        PBGameVars.ballTargetX=-2f;
                                }
                        }
                }
        }
}
```

Notice the if statement that tests if the ball has touched a brick. First, it tests if the y-axis position of the ball (the upper-left corner) is greater than the y-axis position of the brick minus 0.25. This is because the y-axis position of the brick is the upper-left corner of the brick; but we want to see if the ball has hit the bottom of the brick, so we subtract the height of the brick from its y-axis position to get the y-axis position of the bottom.

If the ball hits a brick, the isDestroyed flag of the brick is set to true. As you have seen from the drawBricks() method, any brick that has the isDestroyed flag set to true is not drawn. Therefore, on the next iteration of the game loop, the brick that has been hit will not be drawn and it will disappear from the game screen.

After the brick is destroyed, the ball bounces off of it. Therefore, you now need to calculate the ball's angle of deflection. Luckily for you, all of the bricks lie at 90-degree angles and the angle of attack for the ball is always going to be (roughly) 45 degrees. This gives you a very clean and consistent angle of deflection. In fact, all you have to do to deflect the ball correctly is set the y-axis value to the inverse sign of itself.

> **Tip**   The angle of attack is the angle at which the ball bounces off of an object and continues on the game screen. In real-world physics, a ball bounces off a flat object set to a 90-degree angle at an angle inverse to the angle at which it approached the object. Therefore, a ball approaching a flat, 90-degree angle object at a 30-degree angle would bounce off of it at a 60-degree angle. To avoid the need for having to conduct a full physics lesson, the ball in Prison Break is always going to travel at a 45-degree angle, and every surface is going to be at a 90-degree angle. This way, every time the ball is deflected, it does so at a 45-degree angle.

Finally, you need to set the target for the ball. This was not discussed in the last chapter, but you are cheating a little to get the ball moving. By using the ballTargetX variable, you are giving the ball an x-axis value to "aim for" as it moves. This allows you to easily keep it on course. If the ball is moving right, the target is on the positive side of the x-axis; if the ball is moving left, the target is on the negative side of the x-axis.

When the ball has a collision, it is going to bounce; therefore, the target needs to flip to get the ball moving in the opposite direction.

The final section of the collision detection method tests to see if the ball has hit the player paddle. You will notice that the tests performed against the bricks, as well as the deflections, are also applied to the paddle.

```
if((ball.posY - .25f<=.5f)
&& (ball.posX+.25f>PBGameVars.playerBankPosX )
&& (ball.posX<PBGameVars.playerBankPosX+1.50f)){
        PBGameVars.ballTargetY=PBGameVars.ballTargetY * -1f;
        if(PBGameVars.ballTargetX == -2f){
                PBGameVars.ballTargetX=5f;
        }else{
                PBGameVars.ballTargetX=-2f;
        }
}
if(ball.posX<0 || ball.posX+.25f>3.75f)
```

```
        {
                PBGameVars.ballTargetX = PBGameVars.ballTargetX * -1f;
        }
    }
```

Let's take a look at the finished method in context.

> **Tip**   If you want to tweak the collision detection system, change the detection on the
> ball using the y-axis position to use the y-position minus 0.125. This will give you a
> detection point that is closer to the top of the ball. I used the corner of the ball in the
> preceding code to destroy more bricks simultaneously and clear the screen faster.

The Finished PBGameRenderer

Listing 6-1 shows the finished PBGameRenderer. The collision detection method
and the call to it are bolded to make them easier to see.

Listing 6-1. PBGameRenderer

```
package com.jfdimarzio;

import javax.microedition.khronos.egl.EGLConfig;
import javax.microedition.khronos.opengles.GL10;

import android.opengl.GLSurfaceView.Renderer;

public class PBGameRenderer implements Renderer{

    private PBBackground background = new PBBackground();
    private PBPlayer player1 = new PBPlayer();
    private PBBall ball = new PBBall();
    private PBTextures textureLoader;
    private int[] spriteSheets = new int[3];
    private int numberOfRows = 4;
    private PBWall wall;

    private long loopStart = 0;
    private long loopEnd = 0;
    private long loopRunTime = 0 ;

    private float bgScroll1;
```

```java
@Override
public void onDrawFrame(GL10 gl) {
    // TODO Auto-generated method stub
    loopStart = System.currentTimeMillis();
    // TODO Auto-generated method stub
    try {
        if (loopRunTime < PBGameVars.GAME_THREAD_FPS_SLEEP){
            Thread.sleep(PBGameVars.GAME_THREAD_FPS_SLEEP -
            loopRunTime);
        }
    } catch (InterruptedException e) {
        // TODO Auto-generated catch block
        e.printStackTrace();
    }
    gl.glClear(GL10.GL_COLOR_BUFFER_BIT | GL10.GL_DEPTH_BUFFER_BIT);

    drawBackground1(gl);
    movePlayer1(gl);
    drawBricks(gl);
    moveBall(gl);
    detectCollisions();
    loopEnd = System.currentTimeMillis();
    loopRunTime = ((loopEnd - loopStart));
}

@Override
public void onSurfaceChanged(GL10 gl, int width, int height) {
    // TODO Auto-generated method stub
    gl.glViewport(0, 0, width,height);

    gl.glMatrixMode(GL10.GL_PROJECTION);
    gl.glLoadIdentity();

    gl.glOrthof(0f, 1f, 0f, 1f, -1f, 1f);
}

@Override
public void onSurfaceCreated(GL10 gl, EGLConfig arg1) {
    // TODO Auto-generated method stub
    initializeBricks();
    textureLoader = new PBTextures(gl);
    spriteSheets = textureLoader.loadTexture(gl, PBGameVars.BRICK_
    SHEET, PBGameVars.context, 1);

    gl.glEnable(GL10.GL_TEXTURE_2D);
    gl.glClearDepthf(1.0f);
    gl.glEnable(GL10.GL_DEPTH_TEST);
    gl.glDepthFunc(GL10.GL_LEQUAL);
```

```java
        background.loadTexture(gl,PBGameVars.BACKGROUND, PBGameVars.context);
        player1.loadTexture(gl,PBGameVars.PADDLE, PBGameVars.context);
}

private void drawBackground1(GL10 gl){

        gl.glMatrixMode(GL10.GL_MODELVIEW);
        gl.glLoadIdentity();
        gl.glPushMatrix();
        gl.glScalef(1f, 1f, 1f);

        background.draw(gl);
        gl.glPopMatrix();
        gl.glLoadIdentity();
}

private void initializeBricks(){
        wall=new PBWall(numberOfRows);
}

private void drawBricks(GL10 gl){
        for (int x=0; x<wall.rows.length; x++)
        {
            for(int y=0; y<wall.rows[x].bricks.length; y++)
            {
                if(!wall.rows[x].bricks[y].isDestroyed)
                {
                    switch (wall.rows[x].bricks[y].brickType){
                        case PBGameVars.BRICK_BLUE:

                            gl.glMatrixMode(GL10.GL_MODELVIEW);
                            gl.glLoadIdentity();
                            gl.glPushMatrix();
                            gl.glScalef(.25f, .25f, 1f);
                            gl.glTranslatef(wall.rows[x].bricks[y].posX,
                            wall.rows[x].bricks[y].posY, 0f);

                            gl.glMatrixMode(GL10.GL_TEXTURE);
                            gl.glLoadIdentity();
                            gl.glTranslatef(0.50f, 0.25f, 0.0f);
                            wall.rows[x].bricks[y].draw(gl,spriteSheets);
                            gl.glPopMatrix();
                            gl.glLoadIdentity();
                            break;
                        case PBGameVars.BRICK_BROWN:

                            gl.glMatrixMode(GL10.GL_MODELVIEW);
                            gl.glLoadIdentity();
                            gl.glPushMatrix();
```

```
                        gl.glScalef(.25f, .25f, 1f);

                        gl.glTranslatef(wall.rows[x].bricks[y].posX,
                        wall.rows[x].bricks[y].posY, 0f);

                        gl.glMatrixMode(GL10.GL_TEXTURE);
                        gl.glLoadIdentity();
                        gl.glTranslatef(0.0f, 0.50f, 0.0f);
                        wall.rows[x].bricks[y].draw(gl, spriteSheets);
                        gl.glPopMatrix();
                        gl.glLoadIdentity();
                        break;
                case PBGameVars.BRICK_DARK_GRAY:

                        gl.glMatrixMode(GL10.GL_MODELVIEW);
                        gl.glLoadIdentity();
                        gl.glPushMatrix();
                        gl.glScalef(.25f, .25f, 1f);

                        gl.glTranslatef(wall.rows[x].bricks[y].posX,
                        wall.rows[x].bricks[y].posY, 0f);

                        gl.glMatrixMode(GL10.GL_TEXTURE);
                        gl.glLoadIdentity();
                        gl.glTranslatef(0.25f,0.25f , 0.0f);
                        wall.rows[x].bricks[y].draw(gl, spriteSheets);
                        gl.glPopMatrix();
                        gl.glLoadIdentity();
                        break;
                case PBGameVars.BRICK_GREEN:

                        gl.glMatrixMode(GL10.GL_MODELVIEW);
                        gl.glLoadIdentity();
                        gl.glPushMatrix();
                        gl.glScalef(.25f, .25f, 1f);

                        gl.glTranslatef(wall.rows[x].bricks[y].posX,
                        wall.rows[x].bricks[y].posY, 0f);

                        gl.glMatrixMode(GL10.GL_TEXTURE);
                        gl.glLoadIdentity();
                        gl.glTranslatef(0.0f, 0.25f,0.0f);
                        wall.rows[x].bricks[y].draw(gl, spriteSheets);
                        gl.glPopMatrix();
                        gl.glLoadIdentity();
                        break;
                case PBGameVars.BRICK_LITE_GRAY:

                        gl.glMatrixMode(GL10.GL_MODELVIEW);
                        gl.glLoadIdentity();
```

```
gl.glPushMatrix();
gl.glScalef(.25f, .25f, 1f);

gl.glTranslatef(wall.rows[x].bricks[y].posX,
wall.rows[x].bricks[y].posY, 0f);

gl.glMatrixMode(GL10.GL_TEXTURE);
gl.glLoadIdentity();
gl.glTranslatef(0.25f, 0.0f, 0.0f);
wall.rows[x].bricks[y].draw(gl, spriteSheets);
gl.glPopMatrix();
gl.glLoadIdentity();
break;
case PBGameVars.BRICK_PURPLE:

gl.glMatrixMode(GL10.GL_MODELVIEW);
gl.glLoadIdentity();
gl.glPushMatrix();
gl.glScalef(.25f, .25f, 1f);

gl.glTranslatef(wall.rows[x].bricks[y].posX,
wall.rows[x].bricks[y].posY, 0f);

gl.glMatrixMode(GL10.GL_TEXTURE);
gl.glLoadIdentity();
gl.glTranslatef(0.50f, 0.0f, 0.0f);
wall.rows[x].bricks[y].draw(gl, spriteSheets);
gl.glPopMatrix();
gl.glLoadIdentity();
break;
case PBGameVars.BRICK_RED:

gl.glMatrixMode(GL10.GL_MODELVIEW);
gl.glLoadIdentity();
gl.glPushMatrix();
gl.glScalef(.25f, .25f, 1f);

gl.glTranslatef(wall.rows[x].bricks[y].posX,
wall.rows[x].bricks[y].posY, 0f);

gl.glMatrixMode(GL10.GL_TEXTURE);
gl.glLoadIdentity();
gl.glTranslatef(0.0f, 0.0f, 0.0f);
wall.rows[x].bricks[y].draw(gl, spriteSheets);
gl.glPopMatrix();
gl.glLoadIdentity();
break;
default:
```

```
                              gl.glMatrixMode(GL10.GL_MODELVIEW);
                              gl.glLoadIdentity();
                              gl.glPushMatrix();
                              gl.glScalef(.25f, .25f, 1f);

                              gl.glTranslatef(wall.rows[x].bricks[y].posX,
                              wall.rows[x].bricks[y].posY, 0f);

                              gl.glMatrixMode(GL10.GL_TEXTURE);
                              gl.glLoadIdentity();
                              gl.glTranslatef(0.0f, 0.0f, 0.0f);
                              wall.rows[x].bricks[y].draw(gl, spriteSheets);
                              gl.glPopMatrix();
                              gl.glLoadIdentity();
                              break;
                    }
                }
            }
        }
    }

    private void moveBall(GL10 gl){
        gl.glMatrixMode(GL10.GL_MODELVIEW);
        gl.glLoadIdentity();
        gl.glPushMatrix();
        gl.glScalef(.25f, .25f, 1f);

        ball.posX+= (float) ((PBGameVars.ballTargetX - ball.posX )/
        (ball.posY / (PBGameVars.ballTargetY )));

        ball.posY -=PBGameVars.ballTargetY * 3;

        gl.glTranslatef(ball.posX, ball.posY, 0f);
        gl.glMatrixMode(GL10.GL_TEXTURE);
        gl.glLoadIdentity();
        gl.glTranslatef(0.0f,0.0f, 0.0f);
        ball.draw(gl,spriteSheets);
        gl.glPopMatrix();
        gl.glLoadIdentity();
    }

    private void movePlayer1(GL10 gl){
        gl.glMatrixMode(GL10.GL_MODELVIEW);
        gl.glLoadIdentity();
        gl.glPushMatrix();
        gl.glScalef(.25f, .25f, 1f);

        if (PBGameVars.playerAction == PBGameVars.PLAYER_MOVE_LEFT_1
        &&PBGameVars.playerBankPosX>0)
```

```java
        {
            PBGameVars.playerBankPosX = PBGameVars.playerBankPosX -
            PBGameVars.PLAYER_MOVE_SPEED;
        }
        else if(PBGameVars.playerAction == PBGameVars.PLAYER_MOVE_RIGHT_1
        && PBGameVars.playerBankPosX < 2.5)
        {
            PBGameVars.playerBankPosX = PBGameVars.playerBankPosX +
            PBGameVars.PLAYER_MOVE_SPEED;
        }
        gl.glTranslatef(PBGameVars.playerBankPosX, .5f, 0f);
        gl.glMatrixMode(GL10.GL_TEXTURE);
        gl.glLoadIdentity();
        gl.glTranslatef(0.0f,0.0f, 0.0f);
        player1.draw(gl);
        gl.glPopMatrix();
        gl.glLoadIdentity();
}

private void detectCollisions(){
    if(ball.posY <= 0){
    //GameOver
    }

    for (int x = 0; x < wall.rows.length; x++)
    {
    for(int y = 0; y < wall.rows[x].bricks.length; y++)
    {
        if(!wall.rows[x].bricks[y].isDestroyed)
        {
            if (((ball.posY > wall.rows[x].bricks[y].posY - .25f)
            && (ball.posY < wall.rows[x].bricks[y].posY)
            && (ball.posX + .25f > wall.rows[x].bricks[y].posX)
            && (ball.posX < wall.rows[x].bricks[y].posX + 1.50f)))
            {
                wall.rows[x].bricks[y].isDestroyed = true;
                PBGameVars.ballTargetY = PBGameVars.ballTargetY * -1f;
                if(PBGameVars.ballTargetX == -2f){
                    PBGameVars.ballTargetX = 5f;
                }else{
                    PBGameVars.ballTargetX = -2f;
                }
            }
        }
    }
    }
}

if((ball.posY - .25f <= .5f)
&& (ball.posX + .25f > PBGameVars.playerBankPosX )
```

```
    && (ball.posX < PBGameVars.playerBankPosX + 1.50f)){
        PBGameVars.ballTargetY = PBGameVars.ballTargetY * -1f;
        if(PBGameVars.ballTargetX == -2f){
            PBGameVars.ballTargetX = 5f;
        }else{
            PBGameVars.ballTargetX = -2f;
        }
    }
    if(ball.posX < 0 || ball.posX + .25f > 3.75f)
    {
        PBGameVars.ballTargetX = PBGameVars.ballTargetX * -1f;
    }
    }
}
```

Compile and run your game. You should now be able to play a fairly complete version of your game and break some bricks.

Summary

In this chapter, you learned how to make a basic collision detection system and add it to your game. This gave you a fairly complete version of your game. In the next chapter of the book, we explore several ways to keep score.

Chapter 7

Keeping Score

In the last chapter, you learned how to implement a basic collision detection system in your Prison Break game. This collision detection system allowed you to test for any collisions between the game ball and the bricks or the paddle. It is now time to add the finishing touch to the game.

Most arcade-style games feature a scoring component. Whether it is a direct score or a ranking that correlates to how a level was finished, the score is what lets the player know how he played compared to other players.

In this chapter, you take a look at two possible ways to keep score in Prison Break. The first method adds a specific number of points to the player's score for each brick broken. The second method awards the player a number of points for each complete row of bricks eliminated.

Creating the Scoring Method

To keep score, you first need to add a new method to the PBGameRenderer() that will track the player's score. This method advances the score as you call it.

How will the score be written out to the screen? You create three small vertices following the methods outlined in Chapter 4 and Chapter 5 for making the background, bricks, ball, and paddle. Because we have gone through this procedure four times already, it will not be repeated again here.

Create a new class called PBScoreTile and place instances of it in the upper right-hand corner of your game screen. Next, add to your project a new spritesheet that contains all of the numbers needed to build a score. This spritesheet is shown in Figure 7-1.

Figure 7-1. ScoreNumbers Spritesheet

Each tile should default to the 0 when drawn. This is accomplished by performing a glTranslatef() to the coordinates of 0,0,0 in the texture matrix.

```
gl.glMatrixMode(GL10.GL_TEXTURE);
gl.glLoadIdentity();
gl.glTranslatef(0.0f, 0.0f, 0.0f);
```

For each point scored, use glTranslatef() to move the spritesheet to the corresponding number. This is best achieved in a loop that continues to add 1 to the current score, move a 9 back to a 0 when needed, and advance to the next scoring tile. Therefore, advance your score to the next number each time the method is called by using glTranslatef() to move to the next 0.25 increment in the spritesheet.

The following is an example in pseudocode:

```
private void advanceScore(){

...

        //advance glTranslatef() to the next image in the sprite sheet
        gl.glMatrixMode(GL10.GL_TEXTURE);
        gl.glLoadIdentity();
        gl.glTranslatef(0.0f, 0.0f, 0.0f);
...

}
```

When you have your scoring method finished, it is time to call it.

In the next section, you learn how to call it per brick.

Scoring per Brick

It is very simple to allow your player to score per brick. All you need to do is modify the detectCollisions() method to advance the score when a brick is taken out of play. Modify your detectCollisions() method (as per the following bolded code) to advance the score each time the player destroys a brick.

```
private void detectCollisions(){
        if(ball.posY <= 0){
        //GameOver
        }

        for (int x = 0; x < wall.rows.length; x++)
        {
                for(int y = 0; y < wall.rows[x].bricks.length; y++)
                {
                        if(!wall.rows[x].bricks[y].isDestroyed)
                        {
                                if (((ball.posY > wall.rows[x].bricks[y].posY - .25f)
                                && (ball.posY < wall.rows[x].bricks[y].posY)
                                && (ball.posX + .25f > wall.rows[x].bricks[y].posX)
                                && (ball.posX < wall.rows[x].bricks[y].posX + 1.50f)))
                                {
                                        wall.rows[x].bricks[y].isDestroyed = true;
                                        advanceScore();
                                        PBGameVars.ballTargetY = PBGameVars.
                                        ballTargetY * -1f;
                                        if(PBGameVars.ballTargetX == -2f){
                                                PBGameVars.ballTargetX = 5f;
                                        }else{
                                                PBGameVars.ballTargetX = -2f;
                                        }
                                }
                        }
                }
        }
...
}
```

To add a bit of variety to the scoring, you can also implement a way to give each brick a different point value. First, modify your advanceScore() method to accept an int value representing the number of points you want to advance the score counter. Then, you can simply pass the brickType of the destroyed brick as the number of points that it is worth, as shown in the following bolded code:

```
private void detectCollisions(){
        if(ball.posY <= 0){
        //GameOver
        }

        for (int x = 0; x < wall.rows.length; x++)
        {
                for(int y = 0; y < wall.rows[x].bricks.length; y++)
                {
                        if(!wall.rows[x].bricks[y].isDestroyed)
                        {
                                if (((ball.posY > wall.rows[x].bricks[y].posY - .25f)
```

```
                    && (ball.posY < wall.rows[x].bricks[y].posY)
                    && (ball.posX + .25f > wall.rows[x].bricks[y].posX)
                    && (ball.posX<wall.rows[x].bricks[y].posX + 1.50f)))
                    {
                        wall.rows[x].bricks[y].isDestroyed = true;
                        advanceScore(wall.rows[x].bricks[y]. brickType);
                        PBGameVars.ballTargetY = PBGameVars.
                        ballTargetY * -1f;
                        if(PBGameVars.ballTargetX == -2f){
                            PBGameVars.ballTargetX = 5f;
                        }else{
                            PBGameVars.ballTargetX = -2f;
                        }
                    }
                }
            }
        }
...
}
```

If you don't want to score your players per brick broken, you can also increment the score per row.

Scoring per Row

When you created the PBWall class, one of the features that you built into it was the ability to specify the number of brick rows you want the user to have to break through. You could, theoretically, instantiate this to hundreds of rows and turn the game into more of an endurance game. In doing so, you could track the number of rows the player has successfully cleared.

> **NOTE**   While it is outside the scope of this chapter, if you wanted to create a new game that contained hundreds of brick rows, you would have to create a method that scrolled the screen when the ball moved above the view port. In pseudocode, this would mean that if ball.posY > 4, then glTranslatef(ball.posY - 2, 0.0f,0.0f) in the projection matrix. The -2 keeps the ball in the center of the screen as it scrolls.

Add a new property named numberOfBricksRemaining to your PBRow. This property will track the number of bricks in the current row. When the counter reaches zero, you can advance the score, as in the following example:

```
public class PBRow {
    public PBBrick[] bricks;
    public int numberOfBricksRemaining = 0;
    public boolean rowIsScored = false;
    private Random brickType = new Random();
    private boolean isRowOdd = false;
    private int numberOfBricks = 0;

        public PBRow(int rowNumber){

        if(rowNumber         2 > 0)
        {
                numberOfBricks = 4;
                numberOfBricksRemaining = 4;
                isRowOdd = true;
        }
        else
        {
                numberOfBricks = 5;
                numberOfBricksRemaining = 5;
                isRowOdd = false;
        }


        bricks = new PBBrick[numberOfBricks];


        for(int x = 0; x < numberOfBricks ; x++)
        {
                bricks[x] = new PBBrick((int) (brickType.nextFloat() * 7));
                if(isRowOdd)
                {
                        bricks[x].posX = x - 2f ;
                        bricks[x].posY = (rowNumber * .25f) + 1 ;
                }
                else
                {
                        bricks[x].posX = x - 2.5f;
                        bricks[x].posY = (rowNumber * .25f) + 1 ;
                }
        }
      }
    }
}
```

> **TIP**   The `rowIsScored` property allows you to track whether or not you have already awarded a score to the cleared row.

This will initially set the number of bricks remaining in the row to the total number of bricks in the row. Then, as you iterate through your collision detection method, you subtract 1 from this property for every destroyed brick. Once the property reaches 0, you call your scoring method.

```
private void detectCollisions(){
        if(ball.posY <= 0){
        //GameOver
        }

        for (int x = 0; x < wall.rows.length; x++)
        {
            for(int y = 0; y < wall.rows[x].bricks.length; y++)
            {
                if(!wall.rows[x].bricks[y].isDestroyed)
                {
                    if (((ball.posY > wall.rows[x].bricks[y].posY- .25f)
                    && (ball.posY < wall.rows[x].bricks[y].posY)
                    && (ball.posX + .25f > wall.rows[x].bricks[y].posX)
                    && (ball.posX < wall.rows[x].bricks[y].posX + 1.50f)))
                    {
                        wall.rows[x].bricks[y].isDestroyed = true;
                        wall.rows[x].numberOfBricksRemaining -=;
                        PBGameVars.ballTargetY = PBGameVars.
                        ballTargetY * -1f;
                        if(PBGameVars.ballTargetX == -2f){
                            PBGameVars.ballTargetX = 5f;
                        }else{
                            PBGameVars.ballTargetX = -2f;
                        }
                    }
                }
            }
            if(wall.rows[x]. numberOfBricksRemaining = 0 && wall.
            rows[x].rowIsScored == false){
            advanceScore();
            wall.rows[x].rowIsScored = true;
            }
        }
    ...
}
```

This is all that is required to create a few different score-taking mechanisms. I am sure that, with a little time, you can implement one that is even more creative.

Summary

In this chapter, you learned how to create three different ways to let your player track and compare his score with that of other players. This is vital to arcade games because it gives your player a greater sense of accomplishment.

In the next (and final) chapter of this book, you will learn how to add new levels to Prison Break.

Chapter 8

Adding New Levels

At this point in the book, you have created a functional arcade game. Prison Break can be used as a template for many other games, and the knowledge that you built in this short case study will help you create compelling arcade-style games.

As it stands, however, Prison Break is a rather short game. This chapter takes you through the theory of adding levels to the game. There are two ways you can add new levels to Prison Break—and most arcade games for that matter. You can hardcode each level into the game (*static leveling*); or you can write the game code in such a way that it reads the level information from an outside, changing source (*dynamic leveling*).

Let's first take a look at the theory behind adding static levels to your game.

Adding Static Levels

If you add a finite number of levels to Prison Break—beyond the one already supplied—you are creating static levels. Much of what you need to create additional Prison Break levels is already built into the game.

First, you should create and add multiple backgrounds to your Prison Break project. This will allow you to call a new background corresponding to the level that the player chooses. To make your life easier, create new variables in the PBGameVars to help call the new background images.

Next, create a new button for levels on your menu. Using Chapter 3 as a guide, add a new button and the listener for it. Then, when the player selects the button corresponding to the level he wants to play, call the game activity as the Start button does now; but also set a variable in the PBGameVars similar to

```
PBGameVars.levelSelected = 5;
```

In the `PBGameRenderer`, you can now change your game load based on the level the player selected. In the loading methods of the game renderer, you can swap out the background image, load a different number of rows, or change the ball to correspond to a different level.

Adding Dynamic Levels

A second option, and a far more labor-intensive one, is to modify the game code to accept the dynamic creation of levels. Modifying the code to use dynamic levels will give your players a more enhanced experience because they can continually add to the game. The key to doing something like this is to use an XML-based level definition sheet. You create a level definition sheet, like that shown in Listing 8-1, which tells your code how to load up your level. Then, using this definition sheet, you are able to create an endless number of levels.

Listing 8-1. Level XML

```
<prisonbreaklevel>
        <levelnumber>5</levelnumber>
        <levelbackground>background5.png</levelbackground>
        <levelwall>
                <numberofrows>6</numberofrows>
        <levelwall>
        <levelball>
                <type>normal</type>
</ prisonbreaklevel >
```

This sheet can be stored on a web server, or downloaded to the game via an update and stored in the Android database. Looking at the information in the sheet, it should be apparent how the code would need to be modified to use it.

When loading the `PBGameRenderer`, your code now opens and reads the definition sheet that corresponds to the level that the player selected. The appropriate definition sheet options are then loaded into game, and the level is created.

Summary

In this, the final chapter of an expert case study on Android arcade games, you learned how to change the Prison Break code to accept the creation of multiple levels.

I sincerely hope you enjoyed this book and that it gave you further insight into the creation of games using the Android platform.

Index

GPSR Compliance
The European Union's (EU) General Product Safety Regulation (GPSR) is a set
of rules that requires consumer products to be safe and our obligations to
ensure this.

If you have any concerns about our products, you can contact us on

ProductSafety@springernature.com

In case Publisher is established outside the EU, the EU authorized
representative is:

Springer Nature Customer Service Center GmbH
Europaplatz 3
69115 Heidelberg, Germany

2 04